In the Kitchen with
FUSTINI'S

Creative Cooking with Extra Virgin Olive Oils and Balsamic Vinegars

Foreword by Dave Denison, Chef/Co-Owner, Amical

Fustini's Oils & Vinegars

Traverse City, Michigan

Published by
Fustini's Oils & Vinegars
Traverse City, Michigan
www.fustinis.com

FUSTINI's is a registered trademark of Second Half Productions, LLC dba Fustini's Oils & Vinegars.

Publisher's Cataloging-in-Publication Data
Milligan, Jim.

    In the kitchen with Fustini's : creative cooking with extra virgin olive oils and balsamic vinegars / Jim Milligan. – Traverse City, MI : Fustini's Oils & Vinegars, 2011.

    p. ; cm.

    ISBN13: 978-0-9846560-0-4

    1. Cooking (Olive oil) 2. Cooking (Vinegar) 3. Cookbooks. I. Title.

TX819.O42 M56 2011
641.6463—dc22   2011938722

FIRST EDITION, Second Printing

Project coordination by Jenkins Group, Inc.
www.BookPublishing.com

Photographers: Brian Confer, Michael Lancashire
Editor: Janice Binkert
Cover and Interior Designer: Heather Shaw

Printed in Malaysia
16 15 14 13 12 • 6 5 4 3 2

To our wonderful customers, who have made Fustini's a joy and a success, and without whom this book would not be possible. It is my hope that these recipes will inspire you to continue on the journey with us, exploring ever more creative ways to nutritionally flavor what we're enjoying every time we sit together at the table.

CONTENTS

I didn't see it coming. It was a recipe so simple with its pinpoint focus, a singular mission of combining two ancient ingredients. Whisk in the interaction of our strongest senses—taste and smell. Add the sight of shimmering stainless steel dispensers, linear and symmetrical in their display. Finish with a dash of art, endless creativity and the ability to connect with people.

We sat and listened as the plan was shared, clearly explained and vividly described. Yet we didn't see the vision. Of course, we've known that extra virgin olive oil and infused balsamic vinegar have been around for thousands of years. We industry professionals come into contact with oil and vinegar on every shift, including it in just about any preparation. How could this be different enough to attract all the others?

The Milligans were preparing to make some pressing decisions. Life was changing, and much like it always does, change brings with it the freedom to flow forth with ideas. The merchandising of extra virgin olive oil (EVOO) along with a variety of vinegars was not new. You see it in every specialty market and grocery store. I mean, how many different types of salad dressing does one truly need? This new, tightly focused venture starting out in a town the size of Traverse City was risky business.

It was difficult to imagine that people walking by would stop in for a sip of Sicilian Lemon Balsamic followed by a chaser of spicy Chipotle EVOO. However, once the tasting started, conversation ensued, and there was no end to the limits of the imagination. The suggestions came streaming out. Vinaigrette dressings aren't just for salads, regardless of the broad creativity. Superb marinades enhance food preparations in a most unique way.

You could serve the 18 Year Traditional Balsamic tossed with strawberries for dessert. We do just that at Amical.

Those of us who toil in bistro kitchens, preparing dishes for hundreds of guests, are not accustomed to retail shopkeepers influencing much of what we do. More often than not, it is the dinner house cook or a star Food Channel chef who determines what the marketplace will offer. Not so this time. The colorful bottles brimming with quality vinegar and olive oil that we had acquired for our kitchen shelf beckoned for attention. It didn't take long for us to answer their call. If you've read this far, it's obvious that you've responded, too.

Start out slowly with Fustini's Tangerine Balsamic on Jicama-Radish Salad. Take a small step up to brushing Smoked Paprika Salmon with Fustini's Persian Lime EVOO. Then hit your stride by adding Fustini's Basil EVOO to Chicken with Mushrooms and Sundried Tomatoes. Sprint to dessert with Peach-Blueberry Cobbler baked with a splash of Fustini's Peach Balsamic. And don't serve butter with that bread!

Go ahead. Try your own Fustini's EVOO and balsamic taste combinations—whisk together a marinade or make unique vinaigrette magic. Enhance a favorite recipe or impress a seasoned kitchen veteran. See what's in it for you. For me, it has been an eye-opener.

Dave Denison
Chef/Co-Owner of Amical
Traverse City

Acknowledgments

I would like to recognize the following people for their contributions to _In the Kitchen with Fustini's_:

The fun, creative and dedicated staff at each of our four Michigan Fustini's stores, who provided solid support. They are the face of Fustini's, doing everything from hauling bottles and products into the stores to hosting guests and constantly generating recipes, pairings and flavoring ideas. Thanks to each of our store managers for their commitment to this project and the engagement of their staff: Liz Lancashire (Traverse City), Charlene Hunt (Petoskey), Denise Walburg (Holland) and Jill Gardner-Bakewell (Ann Arbor).

Our chef, catering, culinary school and restaurant partners in Michigan. Their support of Fustini's is sincerely appreciated and their contributions to this cookbook greatly valued. They include 84 East Food & Spirits, Holland; Aerie, at the Grand Traverse Resort, Acme; Alpenrose Restaurant, Holland; Amical, Traverse City; Blu, Glen Arbor; Grand Traverse Pie Company, Traverse City; Great Lakes Culinary Institute, Traverse City; Hanna Bistro, Traverse City; Julienne Tomatoes, Petoskey; Limonata, Holland; Mediterrano, Ann Arbor; Roast and Toast, Petoskey; Simply Cupcakes, Traverse City; Terrace Inn, Bay View.

Chef Harlan "Pete" Peterson, owner of the acclaimed Tapawingo in Ellsworth for twenty-five years and now private caterer and food consultant, who acted as our professional advisor and food stylist, developed new recipes, and led the team that prepared all the recipes for the photo shoot.

Brian Confer, of Brian Confer Photography, who brought the recipes to life with beautiful images. Brian, a well-known northern Michigan photographer, has a love and understanding of good food and an experienced and expert eye for detail.

Chef Fred Laughlin, director of the Great Lakes Culinary Institute in Traverse City, who generously allowed us to use the kitchens and facilities at GLCI, providing the ideal venue for cooking and photographing the recipes that appear in this book.

Chef Paul Gomes and GLCI student James Bloomfield, who worked side by side with Chef Peterson to prepare and plate the recipes that were photographed for this book.

Dave Denison, chef and co-owner of Amical in Traverse City, as well as a great friend and trusted advisor, who wrote the Foreword.

Jeanne Beers and Sally Stilwill, both of Traverse City, who tested recipes and provided excellent feedback.

Janice Binkert, who served as editor and overall coordinator for this project. She was also involved in recipe development and helped prepare the recipes that were photographed. I distinctly remember our first meeting together. Janice and I immediately connected on this project. She did not waiver one bit. With her writing, editing and organizational experience, she built a solid plan and quickly collected a commitment to execute from all of the different stakeholders. She has a passion for cooking and shares my vision for the prominent role that oils and vinegars can play in the kitchen with their great flavor, versatility and nutrition.

A heartfelt thanks to each of you for your contributions to what may become "the first" Fustini's cookbook.

Jim Milligan
Owner, Fustini's Oils & Vinegars

Introduction

Why would someone open a shop that sells only extra virgin olive oils and balsamic vinegars? And in a small town like Traverse City, Michigan, no less! On the surface, it seems like a crazy idea. But if you think about it in the context of what has been happening in the food world in recent years, it makes perfect sense: the quest for quality over quantity, the trend toward buying seasonal products from local vendors (extra virgin olive oil is in fact a seasonal product), ever-increasing numbers of health-conscious consumers, and a renewed interest in home cooking. Today, people around the globe have fallen in love with olive oil—and as an extension, its perfect complement, balsamic vinegar. Each of these natural and naturally beneficial products has its own charms, but together, they are irresistible.

Fustini's extra virgin olive oils (EVOOs) are imported from artisans and small batch producers worldwide at the peak of freshness. Our infused oils and flavored balsamics offer unique tastes and combinations. Those factors, combined with the concept of inviting guests to taste before buying, educating them about flavor profiles and pairings, and offering high-quality, attractive products—bottled right before their eyes—turned out to be anything but a crazy idea. In fact, it was the right idea at the right time and in the right place.

The response to the original Fustini's in Traverse City, founded in 2008, was strong enough that it was evident this could be a viable business. Three more stores were opened in Michigan within two years—in Petoskey and Holland and in the Kerrytown Market and Shops in Ann Arbor. Almost from the start our customers began asking, "Why don't you do a cookbook?" Eventually, encouraged by the support and enthusiasm we continued to get from them, from professional chefs and from our staff members, we asked ourselves the same thing.

In the Kitchen with Fustini's is the result. In it you will find recipes that range from the simple to the sophisticated, familiar ingredients as well as some that may be new to you, and exciting new flavor combinations. Even beyond its contents, we hope this book will inspire you to experiment with Fustini's oils and vinegars in your own favorite dishes and in new recipes you may encounter elsewhere. Our products are infinitely versatile – they can and do enhance everything from breads to meats to desserts. And so, loyal customers, enthusiastic foodies and passionate cooks, we encourage you to get into the kitchen with them and give your creativity free rein!

A few practical notes about this cookbook:

- You will find a general overview of flavor profiles and pairing ideas for all of the featured EVOOs and balsamics beginning on page 127, as well as page numbers where recipes using them can be found.

- We have also included techniques for using our oils and vinegars on page 125.

- Feel free to substitute different oils and vinegars than those suggested in the recipes, according to your own tastes and intuition.

- When "salt and pepper" are specified in a recipe, unless otherwise specified, we recommend kosher or sea salt and freshly ground pepper. Starting with high-quality ingredients (including our oils and vinegars) is in every case the key to good results in cooking!

- Finally, you may be wondering where the name Fustini's comes from. In Italy, a *fustino* is a stainless steel tank that holds and dispenses olive oil—just like the ones we use in our stores. And of course, the Italians know a thing or two about olive oil…

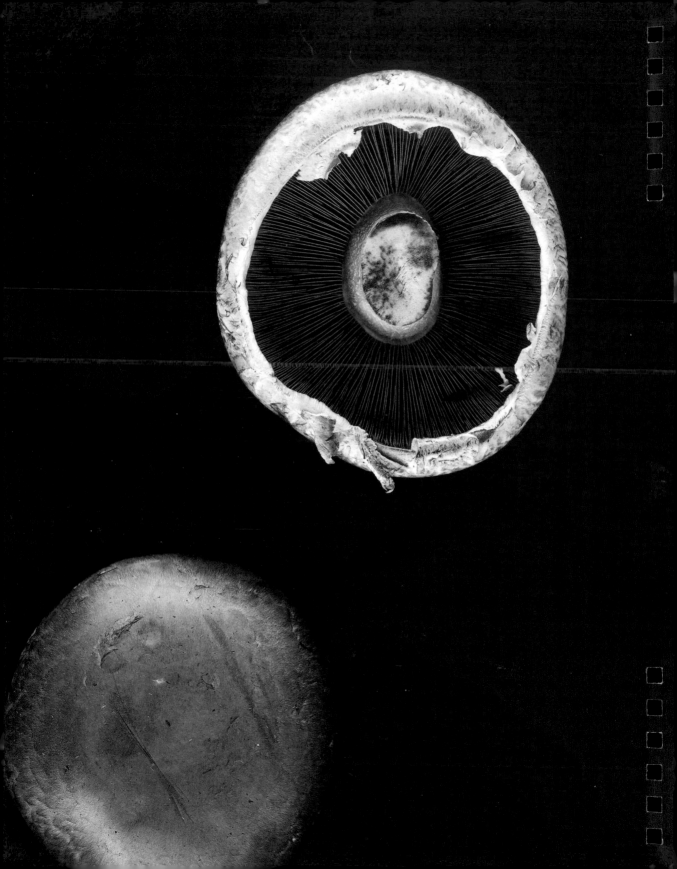

APPETIZERS

Cheese-Filled Crepes
with Asparagus-Tomato Slaw

Asparagus-Tomato Slaw:

1 pound asparagus, cut on the bias into 1-inch pieces

3 large tomatoes, seeded and diced

2 tablespoons Fustini's 12 Year White Balsamic

2 tablespoons Fustini's Meyer Lemon EVOO

salt and pepper to taste

. . . .

In a large skillet, bring about ½ inch of water and 1 teaspoon salt to a boil. Add asparagus, reduce heat to a simmer, and cook 3–5 minutes or until bright green and still somewhat resistant when pierced with the tip of a sharp knife. Allow to cool. Toss with diced tomato. Add Fustini's 12 Year White Balsamic and Fustini's Meyer Lemon EVOO, mix gently, and season with salt and pepper. Chill.

FUSTINI'S
OILS & VINEGARS

MEYER LEMON
NATURAL LEMON FLAVORED
EXTRA VIRGIN OLIVE OIL

GREAT IDEAS:
- Combine with a balsamic for salad dressing or roasting vegetables
- Use to sauté, bake, or grill chicken, shrimp or fish
- Sauté dry rice in Meyer Lemon EVOO until translucent, add liquid, then cook as directed
- Replace other oils in baking

Crepes:

1 cup all-purpose flour

2 eggs

¼ teaspoon salt

½ cup milk

½ cup water

1 tablespoon Fustini's Basil EVOO

2 tablespoons melted butter

1 cup havarti cheese (or other semi-firm cheese of your choice), shredded

· ·

In a large bowl, whisk together the flour, eggs and salt. Gradually add milk and water, stirring to combine. Batter will be thin. Refrigerate one hour.

Heat a small nonstick skillet to medium hot. Combine Fustini's Basil EVOO and melted butter. Brush pan lightly with oil and butter mixture. Make crepes one at a time, using ¼ cup batter per crepe. Tilt the pan with a circular motion to coat the bottom of the pan with the crepe mixture. Cook about 2 minutes. Loosen with spatula, flip over, and cook the other side, about 1 minute more. Set aside, cover and keep warm until ready to assemble. Repeat procedure with remaining batter.

Assembly:

Divide cheese evenly among crepes and roll up firmly; trim ends of crepes. Cut into ½-inch slices. Top with some of the asparagus-tomato slaw.

Adapted from a recipe contributed by Alpenrose Restaurant, Holland

3

SERVINGS VARY

Fustini's Salsa with Spicy Pita Chips

Salsa:

8 fresh ripe tomatoes, seeded and diced

½ red onion, diced

1 small bunch cilantro, finely chopped

¼ cup Fustini's Tangerine Balsamic, more or less to taste

¼ cup Fustini's Chipotle EVOO, more or less to taste

⅛ cup Fustini's Jalapeño Balsamic, more or less to taste

Ssalt and pepper to taste

[or substitute 2 14½-ounce cans diced tomatoes, well drained

. . . .

Mix all ingredients, then season with salt and pepper and chill. The flavors taste even better the next day, so make a day in advance if possible. Serve with spicy pita chips (recipe follows).

Spicy Pita Chips:

5 whole wheat pita rounds

¼ cup Fustini's Garlic EVOO

2 teaspoons coarse salt

2 teaspoons cumin

⅛ teaspoon chili powder

. . . .

Preheat oven to 375 degrees. Cut each pita round into six triangles like a pie, leaving top and bottom attached. Brush with Fustini's Garlic EVOO. Place pita triangles on a rimmed sheet pan lined with parchment paper or foil. Mix salt, cumin and chili powder. Sprinkle on pita triangles.

Bake 5 minutes or until golden brown and crispy.

Contributed by Fustini's of Traverse City

5

Lettuce Wraps with Turkey and Ginger-Honey Rice

1–2 heads Bibb lettuce

¾ cup onion, chopped

1 pound ground turkey

2 tablespoons Fustini's Cilantro and Onion EVOO

¼ cup Fustini's Ginger and Honey Balsamic

3 tablespoons fresh mint

4 teaspoons fish sauce

2 tablespoons fresh cilantro

½ teaspoon red pepper flakes

2 tablespoons Fustini's Persian Lime EVOO

Ginger-Honey Rice (recipe follows)

Separate 12 smaller inner lettuce leaves; wash and dry thoroughly. Set aside.

Heat 2 tablespoons Fustini's Cilantro and Onion EVOO in a skillet, add onion and sweat until translucent. Add ground turkey and cook until no longer pink. Drain fat and return meat to pan. Add remaining ingredients and mix well.

To serve, place turkey and rice in lettuce leaf; wrap and eat by hand.

Ginger-Honey Rice:

2 cups Basmati rice

3 cups water

2 tablespoons Fustini's Ginger and Honey Balsamic, or more to taste

Cook rice according to directions, adding Fustini's Ginger and Honey Balsamic just before end of cooking. Mix well.

Contributed by Fustini's of Traverse City

Peaches with Prosciutto and Basil

3 freestone peaches, peeled and cut into 8 wedges each

¼ teaspoon sugar

½ teaspoon Fustini's Sherry Reserva Vinegar

pinch of ground cumin

¼ pound prosciutto, thinly sliced

24 small basil leaves

¼ cup Fustini's Vanilla Bean Balsamic, reduced by half

. . . .

Toss together peaches, sugar, Fustini's Sherry Reserva Vinegar and cumin; let stand 10 minutes.

Cut prosciutto slices in half lengthwise and wrap each piece around a wedge of peach. Top with a basil leaf and secure with a toothpick. Drizzle lightly with Fustini's Vanilla Bean Balsamic reduction.

Contributed by Fustini's of Petoskey

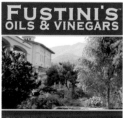

SHERRY RESERVA VINEGAR

GREAT IDEAS:
- Combine with Persian Lime EVOO for dressing taco salad
- Combine with Provençal Herbes EVOO for a savory salad dressing
- Add to gazpacho for enhanced flavor
- Marinate olives in Sherry Reserva Vinegar, Sweet Hojiblanca EVOO, fresh orange juice, lemon zest, garlic and thyme
- Great mixed with our 18 Year Traditional Balsamic to add a sharper note

Potato and Rosemary Pizza

SERVINGS VARY

4 medium premade pizza dough rounds or any recipe yielding 4 medium pizza dough rounds

2–3 medium potatoes

salt to taste

Fustini's Leccino or Frantoio EVOO, for brushing

2 6-inch rosemary sprigs, picked and chopped

1 cup Asiago or Parmigiano Reggiano cheese, shaved or shredded

Fustini's White Truffle EVOO, for finishing

. . . .

Preheat oven to 400 degrees.

Flatten out pizza rounds into 6-inch circles and place on a lightly oiled sheet pan.

Peel and slice potatoes into very thin rounds, salt them and set aside for 10 minutes. Rinse potatoes and pat dry. Arrange potatoes on top of pizza, brush with Leccino or Frantoio EVOO and bake 10 minutes.

Sprinkle pizzas with chopped rosemary and cheese. Bake until crust is cooked through (about 10 more minutes).

Cut each pizza into 6 pieces and drizzle with Fustini's White Truffle EVOO.

Adapted from a recipe contributed by Hanna Bistro, Traverse City

Poached Shrimp with Lemon-Horseradish Dipping Sauce

Shrimp:

2 cups dry white wine

6 whole black peppercorns

½ cup Fustini's Sicilian Lemon Balsamic

1 bay leaf

pinch salt

16 uncooked, unpeeled large shrimp

Fill medium bowl with ice water; set aside. Combine 2 cups water, wine and next 4 ingredients (through salt) in medium saucepan. Bring to a boil. Add shrimp; reduce heat to low, cover and poach just until shells are pink and shrimp are opaque in center, 3–4 minutes. Using a slotted spoon, transfer shrimp to ice water; reserve poaching liquid. Drain, peel and devein shrimp, leaving tails intact.

Dipping Sauce:

½ cup crème fraîche or sour cream

2 tablespoons chopped fresh chives

2 teaspoons prepared horseradish

2 tablespoons Fustini's Sicilian Lemon Balsamic

½ lemon, zest

Salt and pepper to taste

Whole fresh chives for garnish

Boil poaching liquid until reduced to generous 2 tablespoons, about 20 minutes. Strain and cool. Mix crème fraîche, chopped chives, horseradish and 1 tablespoon reduced poaching liquid in small bowl. Season sauce with salt and pepper.

Shrimp and sauce can be made one day ahead. Store and cover separately; chill.

Spoon dipping sauce into 4 short glasses; arrange 4 shrimp on rim of each glass. Garnish with whole fresh chives.

SERVES 4

Roasted Portobello Mushrooms with Halloumi Cheese and Red Pepper Coulis

4 large portobello mushrooms, stems removed

2 large red bell peppers, quartered, ribs and seeds removed

4 tablespoons Fustini's Porcini Mushroom EVOO

3 tablespoons Fustini's 12 Year Traditional Balsamic, divided

1 teaspoon dried red pepper flakes

4 tablespoons Fustini's Koroneiki EVOO, divided

1 pound halloumi cheese, cut into ¼-inch thick slices

salt and pepper to taste

Basil Pesto (recipe follows)

2 tablespoons pine nuts

2 lemons, thinly sliced

. . . .

Preheat oven to 450 degrees.

Clean mushrooms by wiping with a damp paper towel. Wash and dry peppers.

Combine Fustini's Porcini EVOO, 2 tablespoons Fustini's 12 Year Traditional Balsamic, dried red pepper flakes and salt to make a vinaigrette. Brush mushrooms and peppers with vinaigrette. Roast until beginning to brown, about 10 minutes for mushrooms and 15–20 minutes for peppers.

Combine roasted peppers, 2 tablespoons Fustini's Koroneiki EVOO and 1 tablespoon Fustini's 12 Year Traditional Balsamic in a blender or food processor and process to a smooth coulis. Season with salt and pepper.

Brush halloumi slices lightly with 2 tablespoons Fustini's Koroneiki EVOO and sear on a hot griddle or in a nonstick pan about 2 minutes per side or until golden brown. Slice mushrooms into four pieces.

Divide roasted red pepper coulis among four plates. Alternate mushroom slices with halloumi on top of coulis on each plate. Drizzle with pesto, sprinkle with toasted pine nuts, and garnish with thin slices of lemon.

Basil Pesto:

5 cups basil leaves, tightly packed

4 garlic cloves, minced

2 tablespoons pine nuts

¼ cup Parmigiano Reggiano, grated

⅓ cup Fustini's Picholine EVOO or Basil EVOO

salt to taste

Combine basil, garlic, pine nuts and cheese in a food processor. Chop coarsely using pulse setting. With food processor running, slowly add Fustini's Picholine EVOO in a steady stream until mixture is smooth. Season to taste with salt.

Adapted from a recipe contributed by Mediterrano, Ann Arbor

GREAT IDEAS:
- Use to sauté or roast vegetables
- Drizzle on pasta with prosciutto and caramelized red onions
- Brush on toast or English muffins
- Combine with Cherry Balsamic for spinach salad dressing
- Combine with Fig or Cherry Balsamic to marinate pork tenderloin or chicken
- Sauté chicken with Tunisian Harissa EVOO and Sicilian Lemon Balsamic

FUSTINI'S
OILS & VINEGARS

PORCINI MUSHROOM
NATURAL PORCINI MUSHROOM FLAVORED
EXTRA VIRGIN OLIVE OIL

Roasted Red Pepper and Asparagus Crostini

1 whole garlic bulb

1 rosemary sprig

2 red bell peppers

Fustini's Tuscan Herb EVOO

salt and pepper to taste

1 French baguette

24 asparagus tips (reserve stalks for another use)

2 teaspoons Fustini's 18 Year Traditional Balsamic, plus more for drizzling

Preheat oven to 400 degrees.

Slice top off whole garlic bulb. Place bulb on a square of foil. Drizzle with Fustini's Tuscan Herb EVOO, a pinch of salt, a grind of fresh pepper and 1 rosemary spring. Wrap foil around bulb. Cut peppers in half; remove ribs and seeds. Place on sheet of foil or baking sheet. Brush with Fustini's Tuscan Herb EVOO. Roast garlic bulb and pepper halves 25–30 minutes or until garlic is soft and peppers begin to char. Set aside to cool.

Lower oven temperature to 350 degrees. To make crostini, slice baguette into ¾-inch slices. Place on ungreased baking sheet. Brush with Fustini's Tuscan Herb EVOO; turn over and repeat. Bake 15 minutes or until golden. Meanwhile, in a large skillet, bring about ½ inch of water and salt to a boil. Add asparagus, reduce heat to a simmer, and cook for 3–5 minutes or until bright green and still somewhat resistant when pierced with the tip of a sharp knife; drain and cool.

Squeeze roasted garlic from bulbs into a small bowl; spread on crostini. Slice roasted red pepper into thin strips; place in small bowl. Drizzle with 2 teaspoons Fustini's 18 Year Traditional Balsamic. Mix gently until peppers are coated. Place a few peppers on crostini and top with 2 steamed asparagus tips. Drizzle with a little Fustini's 18 Year Traditional Balsamic. Season to taste with salt and pepper.

Contributed by Fustini's of Petoskey

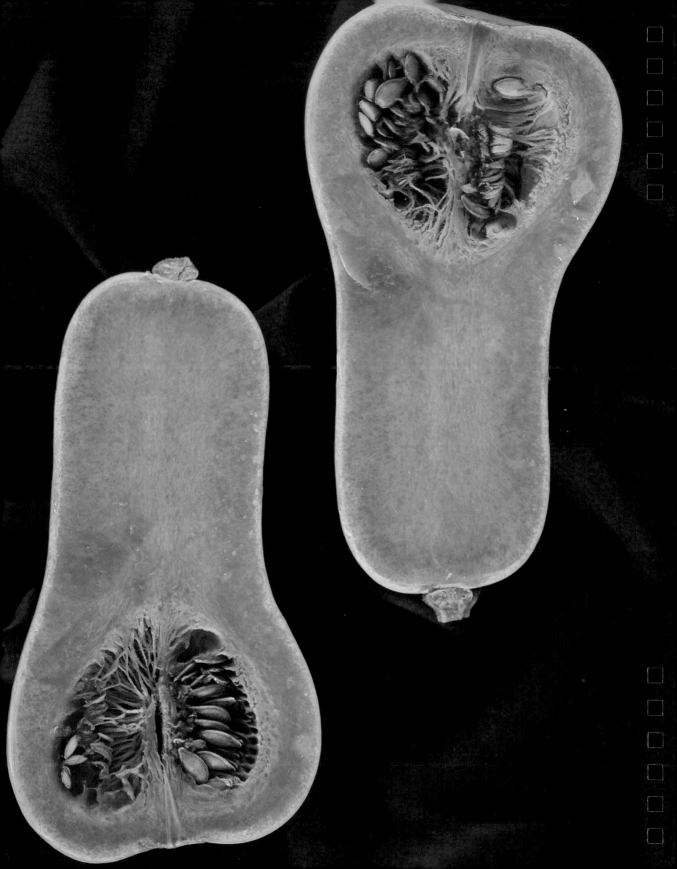

SOUPS & BREADS

• GAZPACHO WITH GARLIC CROUTONS •
18

• SUMMER VEGETABLE SOUP WITH BARLEY •
21

• SUNDRIED TOMATO AND CHEESE BREAD •
22

• SOFT BAGUETTES OR DINNER ROLLS •
25

• ROASTED BUTTERNUT SQUASH AND ANCHO CHILE BISQUE •
26

• CHIPOTLE PEPITAS •
28

• TUSCAN HERB BREAD •
29

• CURRIED LENTIL SOUP •
30

• BROCCOLI AND WHITE CHEDDAR SOUP
WITH GARLIC AND TARRAGON •
33

Gazpacho with Garlic Croutons

SERVES 6

Gazpacho:

1 tablespoon Fustini's Sherry Reserva Vinegar

½ cup Fustini's Manzanillo EVOO

1½–2 pounds large, ripe, flavorful tomatoes, chopped

1 medium Spanish onion, diced

2 garlic cloves, minced

1 red and 1 green bell pepper, diced (reserve 1 tablespoon of each for garnish)

1 hothouse cucumber, seeded and diced (reserve 1 tablespoon for garnish)

1 thick slice day-old crusty white bread, softened in water

1 jalapeño pepper, ribs removed, seeded and minced

1 small bunch cilantro, 4 sprigs reserved for garnish, rest roughly chopped

salt and pepper to taste

4 green onions, light green and white parts only, thinly sliced, for garnish

....

Place all ingredients up to and including cilantro in a blender or food processor and pulse until fairly smooth. Season to taste with salt and pepper. Chill at least 1 hour or overnight.

To serve, put an ice cube in a chilled bowl, pour cold soup over and garnish with diced peppers and cucumbers, green onions, cilantro sprig and garlic croutons (recipe follows).

Continued...

Croutons:

2 slices day-old crusty white bread, cut into cubes

2 tablespoons Fustini's Garlic EVOO

....

Preheat oven to 350 degrees.

Spread bread cubes out on a parchment-lined rimmed baking sheet and brush with Fustini's Garlic EVOO. Bake 25–30 minutes, or until golden brown.

FUSTINI'S
OILS & VINEGARS

MANZANILLO
EXTRA VIRGIN OLIVE OIL

GREAT IDEAS:
- Sear tuna steaks in pan on both sides, remove from pan: reduce heat, then deglaze pan with Peach Balsamic and drizzle glaze over tuna
- Combine with Asian Blackberry Balsamic for a spinach and goat cheese salad dressing

FUSTINI'S
OILS & VINEGARS

GARLIC
NATURAL GARLIC FLAVORED
EXTRA VIRGIN OLIVE OIL

GREAT IDEAS:
- Combine with 18 Year Traditional or Oregano Balsamic to drizzle on salads
- Combine with Peach or Golden Pineapple Balsamic for a chicken and pork marinade
- Combine with equal parts of Espresso Bean Balsamic and Tunisian Harissa EVOO for a flank steak or chicken marinade
- Use alone or with any Fustini's balsamic for roasting vegetables or bread dipping

Summer Vegetable Soup with Barley

SERVES 6 – 8

4 tablespoons Fustini's Picual EVOO

1 medium onion, chopped

2 garlic cloves, minced

3 medium carrots, chopped

1 zucchini, chopped

1 summer squash, chopped

1 cup fresh corn

½ cup fresh green beans

½ head Savoy cabbage, cored, quartered and chopped

2 large ripe tomatoes, cored, seeded and chopped

2 quarts vegetable broth, or more as needed

2 sprigs fresh thyme

1 tablespoon Fustini's Oregano Balsamic

½ cup quick-cooking barley

1 bunch fresh chives, chopped finely for garnish

. . . .

Heat Fustini's Picual EVOO in a Dutch oven or stockpot until hot but not smoking. Add onion and sauté until translucent. Add carrots and sauté 2 minutes. Add next 6 ingredients (zucchini through cabbage) and sauté, stirring over medium heat until just starting to brown.

Stir in tomatoes, broth and thyme. Bring to a boil, then lower heat and simmer about 30 minutes. Add barley and cook about 10–15 minutes longer. Add more broth as needed. Remove thyme stems and stir in Fustini's Oregano Balsamic. Serve in deep, rimmed soup bowls, garnished with chopped chives.

Sundried Tomato and Cheese Bread

3½ cups cold water

9 cups bread flour

1 cup whole wheat flour

½ cup Fustini's Picual EVOO or Sweet Hojiblanca EVOO

1 tablespoon salt

2 tablespoons instant dry yeast

4½ ounces sundried tomatoes, soaked in warm water for 10 minutes, then diced

3 tablespoons garlic, coarsely chopped

2 tablespoons fresh rosemary, chopped

⅓ cup Asiago cheese, cut in small dice

⅓ cup Parmigiano Reggiano, shredded

. . . .

Preheat oven to 420 degrees.

Pour cold water into bowl of a stand mixer with dough hook attachment. Add next 5 ingredients (up to and including yeast) on top of water and mix at speed 1 for 4 minutes. Then mix at speed 2 for an additional 4 minutes.

When dough is mixed, add and mix in tomatoes, garlic, rosemary and cheeses until thoroughly incorporated. It is normal for the dough to be sticky.

Let dough rise in an oiled bowl for 45 minutes or until doubled in bulk. Punch down and fold in thirds similar to a business letter. Let rise another 30 minutes.

Divide dough into five pieces. Shape into rounds and let rest 15 minutes. Shape into oblong loaves, cover with a damp towel, and let rise again about 45 minutes.

Score each loaf 3 times like a baguette and spray lightly with water. Bake on a parchment-lined sheet pan 20–22 minutes.

Both the dough and the finished bread freeze well, so don't hesitate to make the whole quantity. To freeze dough, make a tight ball after the first rise and roll in flour. Then put in an oiled ziplock bag and squeeze out the air. May be frozen up to a month. Bread can be frozen in the same manner (do not oil bag) up to 3 months.

Contributed by the Great Lakes Culinary Institute, Traverse City

GREAT IDEAS:
- Combine with any Fustini's balsamic to marinate or grill chicken or seafood
- Drizzle on rice or pasta or add to oriental rice or noodle soup
- Combine with Basil EVOO to roast or sauté vegetables
- Use as finishing oil for Asian recipes

SWEET HOJIBLANCA
EXTRA VIRGIN OLIVE OIL

GREAT IDEAS:
- Combine with any Fustini's balsamic for salad dressings or roasting/grilling/sautéing vegetables
- Use in place of other oils for baking
- Great for bread dipping

PICUAL
EXTRA VIRGIN OLIVE OIL

Soft Baguettes or Dinner Rolls

3½ cups cold water

1/8 cup malt syrup

½ cup Fustini's Frantoio EVOO or Sweet Hojiblanca EVOO

1 tablespoon salt

3 tablespoons instant dry yeast

10 cups bread flour

2 cups whole wheat flour

....

Preheat oven to 385 degrees.

Pour cold water into bowl of a stand mixer with dough hook attachment. Add all ingredients on top of water and mix at speed 1 for 11–12 minutes.

Let dough rise in an oiled bowl 1 hour, or until double in bulk. Punch down and shape as desired into baguettes or dinner rolls. If making baguettes, score tops diagonally three times. Cover with a damp towel and let rise again about 40 minutes.

Spray tops of baguettes or rolls lightly with water. Bake for 20–22 minutes for baguettes or 10-12 minutes for rolls, until bread sounds hollow when tapped.

Both the dough and the finished bread freeze well, so don't hesitate to make the whole quantity. To freeze dough, make a tight ball after the first rise and roll in flour. Then put in an oiled ziplock bag and squeeze out the air. May be frozen for up to a month. Bread can be frozen in the same manner (do not oil bag) for up to 3 months.

Contributed by the Great Lakes Culinary Institute, Traverse City

Roasted Butternut Squash and Ancho Chile Bisque

1 butternut squash, halved lengthwise

½ cup Fustini's Blood Orange EVOO, divided

3 Granny Smith apples, 2 cored and sliced thinly, 1 julienned for garnish

1 baking potato, peeled and cut in medium dice

1 ancho chile, rehydrated in boiling water, drained and chopped roughly

½ yellow onion, thinly sliced

2 tablespoons garlic, chopped

2 bay leaves

2 32-ounce cartons chicken broth or vegetable broth (or more as needed)

salt and pepper to taste

1 cup heavy cream, or more as needed

Chipotle Pepitas, optional (recipe follows)

....

Preheat oven to 375 degrees.

Scoop seeds out of squash with a large spoon and brush cut halves and hollow with about ¼ cup Fustini's Blood Orange EVOO. Place squash on a rimmed sheet pan brushed with more EVOO and roast 25–30 minutes, until soft and beginning to caramelize.

When cool enough to handle, scoop squash out of shell and combine with next 6 ingredients (sliced apples through bay leaves) in stockpot. Add enough broth to cover by at least 1 inch and bring to a boil. Reduce to a simmer and cook until all vegetables are tender, stirring occasionally and checking to see if more broth is needed. Meanwhile, make Chipotle Pepitas, if using.

Continued...

Puree soup with an immersion blender, countertop blender or food processor (be careful; liquid will be hot), then push through a strainer. Return to stockpot and season with salt and pepper to taste. Add a cup of cream and heat gently—do not boil. Add more stock or cream to achieve desired thickness. Pour into soup cups or bowls, drizzle with remaining Fustini's Blood Orange EVOO, and top with a fine julienne of green apple and Chipotle Pepitas if desired.

Chipotle Pepitas:

2 tablespoons Fustini's Chipotle EVOO

2 cups raw pumpkin seeds

1 teaspoon fine sea salt

Preheat oven to 325 degrees.

Toss pumpkin seeds with Fustini's Chipotle EVOO and sprinkle with sea salt. Roast on an ungreased baking sheet 15–20 minutes or until golden.

Contributed by Hanna Bistro, Traverse City

GREAT IDEAS:
- Combine with Espresso Bean or Chocolate Balsamic for a great marinade
- Brush on bread instead of butter for grilled cheese
- Combine with Strawberry Balsamic for a spicy, sweet and savory salad dressing
- Combine with Lavender Balsamic for Asian flavor
- Make salsa by combining with Tangerine Balsamic, chopped onions, tomatoes and cilantro for chips, chicken or pork

Tuscan Herb Bread

Photo on page 24

SERVES 6

1⅛ cups warm water

2 teaspoons dry yeast

2 tablespoons sugar

2 teaspoons Seasonello aromatic herbal salt (available at Fustini's)

2 tablespoons Fustini's Tuscan Herb EVOO, plus more for brushing

4 cups flour (approximately)

¼ cup Asiago or Parmigiano Reggiano, grated (optional)

. . . .

Preheat oven to 375 degrees.

Combine warm water, yeast and sugar in a large mixing bowl. Let rest until foamy (about 10 minutes).

Add Seasonello and Fustini's Tuscan Herb EVOO to yeast mixture and stir until salt is dissolved. Mix in flour 1 cup at a time until a sticky dough forms.

Turn dough out onto a well-floured surface and knead until smooth and elastic (add more flour as needed). Form dough into a ball and brush the surface with Fustini's Tuscan Herb EVOO. Return to mixing bowl, cover bowl with plastic wrap and a kitchen towel and let rest in a warm, draft-free area until double in size (about an hour).

Punch dough down, knead a few more times, and form into either 1 large loaf or 2 smaller loaves (baguette style). Place loaves on a lightly oiled baking sheet, score tops, and cover loosely with plastic wrap. Let rest until almost double in size (about 20 minutes). Top loaves with grated Asiago or Parmigiano Reggiano if using. Bake 25–30 minutes or until top is golden brown. Brush top of bread lightly with Fustini's Tuscan herb EVOO and cool on rack.

Note: Can also be made in a bread machine using dough cycle

Contributed by Fustini's of Petoskey

Curried Lentil Soup

1 pound brown or green lentils (about 2¼ cups)

2 tablespoons Fustini's Cilantro and Onion EVOO

1 medium onion, chopped

3 carrots, chopped or sliced

2 stalks celery, chopped or sliced

2 large garlic cloves, pressed or finely chopped

1 teaspoon ground cumin, or to taste

2–4 tablespoons curry powder, or to taste

1 teaspoon chili garlic paste (optional)

1 bay leaf (remove after cooking)

1 14 ½-ounce can diced or coarsely cut tomatoes with juice

3 cups fresh baby spinach leaves

2–3 quarts chicken broth, divided

1 teaspoon fresh thyme leaves, chopped

2 teaspoons Fustini's 12 Year White Balsamic

salt and pepper to taste

1 cup sour cream, for garnish

fresh flat-leaf parsley, chopped, for garnish

. . . .

Rinse and pick through lentils. Set aside.

Sauté onion, carrots and celery over medium heat in Fustini's Cilantro and Onion EVOO. Add garlic, cumin, curry powder, chili-garlic paste (if using) and bay leaf and cook 1–2 minutes, or until fragrant.

Continued...

Stir in tomatoes, spinach and 2 cartons chicken broth and bring to a boil. Add lentils and thyme, return to boil, then lower heat and simmer 35–40 minutes, or until lentils are softened but still hold their shape. Check during cooking and add more broth as needed to achieve desired consistency. Toward end of cooking time, add Fustini's 12 Year White Balsamic and stir. Season to taste with salt and pepper.

Serve garnished with a dollop of sour cream and a sprinkle of parsley.

GREAT IDEAS:
- Combine with any Fustini's citrus EVOO and drizzle on a wedge of lettuce with fresh tomato slices and blue cheese or Gorgonzola cheese
- Combine with Garlic EVOO, drizzle over green beans and serve warm or chilled
- Drizzle over fresh fruit salad
- Brush on any white fish, sprinkle on fresh thyme and bake

GREAT IDEAS:
- Combine with 18 Year Traditional to marinate and grill chicken thighs
- Combine with Jalapeño Balsamic to marinate skirt steaks for fajitas
- Use to roast cauliflower, broccoli, potatoes and asparagus
- Brush on bread for a grilled cheese sandwich

Broccoli and White Cheddar Soup
with Garlic and Tarragon

1 medium onion, chopped

½ cup Fustini's Garlic EVOO, divided

2 large bunches broccoli

6 cloves garlic, smashed and chopped

1 tablespoon fresh tarragon, chopped, plus sprigs for garnish — or substitute 1 teaspoon dried tarragon

1 teaspoon red pepper flakes (optional)

2–2½ quarts (8–10 cups) vegetable broth

¼ cup dry white wine

2 tablespoons fresh lemon juice

1 tablespoon salt, or more to taste

pepper to taste

1 cup sharp white cheddar, grated, divided

. . . .

Remove broccoli florets from stems and cut large pieces into halves or fourths; trim, peel and cut stems about ¼-inch thick.

Sauté onion in ¼ cup Fustini's Garlic EVOO in a stockpot over medium heat until translucent. Add broccoli, garlic, tarragon, 1½ quarts vegetable broth, wine, lemon juice and remaining olive oil and bring to a boil. Reduce heat to a simmer, cover, and cook 30 minutes, stirring occasionally and adding more broth as necessary.

Puree the soup with a handheld immersion blender or transfer to a food processor or blender and puree in batches (be careful; liquid will be hot). Add more broth if necessary to achieve desired consistency. Stir in ½ cup white cheddar until it melts. Season with salt and pepper to taste. Pour into bowls and garnish with remaining white cheddar and sprigs of tarragon.

SALADS & DRESSINGS

SERVES 6

Antipasto Salad with Italian Vinaigrette

4 cups mixed greens (e.g., Bibb lettuce, arugula and mache or mesclun mix)

1 medium red onion, thinly sliced

4–6 slices Genoa salami, cut into thin strips

4–6 slices prosciutto or capicola, cut into thin strips

4 slices provolone, cut into thin strips

½ cup baby bocconcini (pearls)

¼ cup Kalamata olives, pitted

1 cup cherry tomatoes, halved

1 red bell pepper, ribs removed and seeded, cut into thin strips

½ cup marinated artichoke hearts, cut into bite-sized pieces

8 pickled pepperoncini, whole

4–6 fresh basil leaves, chiffonade

1 tablespoon fresh oregano, chopped (or 1 teaspoon dried oregano)

¼ cup Parmigiano Reggiano, grated

. . . .

In a large bowl, mix all ingredients up to and including artichoke hearts. Dress with Italian Vinaigrette (recipe follows). Carefully mix in pepperoncini, then basil and oregano. Sprinkle with Parmigiano Reggiano.

Italian Vinaigrette:

2 tablespoons Fustini's Oregano Balsamic

2 tablespoons Fustini's Pinot Noir Wine Vinegar

2 cloves garlic, pressed or crushed and minced

1 teaspoon Dijon mustard

¼ cup Fustini's Leccino EVOO

salt and pepper to taste

Whisk Fustini's Oregano Balsamic, Fustini's Pinot Noir Wine Vinegar, garlic and mustard in a small bowl; slowly add Fustini's Leccino EVOO and emulsify. Add salt and pepper to taste.

GREAT IDEAS:
- Combine with Blood Orange EVOO and drizzle on a Caprese salad
- Combine with Porcini, Basil or Garlic EVOO, and drizzle over pasta or use as a great salad dressing
- Chop tomatoes and cucumber, drizzle in Oregano Balsamic, and add salt and pepper for savory bruschetta

Asparagus Vinaigrette

1 bunch asparagus (not pencil thin)

1½ teaspoons salt, divided

3 tablespoons Fustini's Pinot Noir Wine Vinegar

½ cup Fustini's Frantoio EVOO

½ yellow bell pepper, small dice

½ orange bell pepper, small dice

½ Italian sweet red pepper, minced

1 bunch scallions

2 tablespoons fresh parsley, finely chopped

pepper, to taste

. . . .

Cut or break woody ends off asparagus. In a large skillet, bring about ½ inch water and 1 teaspoon salt to a boil. Add asparagus, reduce heat to a simmer and cook 3–5 minutes or until bright green and still somewhat resistant when pierced with the tip of a sharp knife. Drain and place in a shallow presentation dish that is at least as long as the asparagus.

To make vinaigrette, place Fustini's Pinot Noir Wine Vinegar in a bowl and slowly add Fustini's Frantoio EVOO as you whisk to emulsify. Whisk in ½ teaspoon salt and pepper to taste. Add peppers, scallions and parsley and mix well. Pour over asparagus and allow to marinate at room temperature about 30 minutes.

Black Bean, Corn and Tomato Salad

Photo on page 60

SERVES 4

1 lime, juice only

2 tablespoons Fustini's Avocado Oil

3 tablespoons Fustini's Jalapeño Balsamic

Salt and pepper to taste

1 16-ounce can black beans, drained and rinsed

4 medium tomatoes, diced (or 12 cherry tomatoes, quartered)

2 cups fresh corn kernels, steamed 3 minutes

½ red onion, chopped

2 garlic cloves, finely chopped

½ bunch cilantro, chopped

1 avocado, diced

1 jalapeño pepper, minced

. . . .

To make dressing, whisk lime juice, Fustini's Avocado Oil and Fustini's Jalapeño Balsamic in a medium bowl; season to taste with salt and pepper. Add remaining ingredients and mix gently. Chill at least 1 hour. Makes an excellent accompaniment to Tequila-Lime Chicken (recipe on page 60).

FUSTINI'S
OILS & VINEGARS

AVOCADO OIL

GREAT IDEAS:
• Use on rice or pasta
• Sauté carrots with Avocado Oil and top with Sicilian Lemon Balsamic to caramelize
• Great for avocado and goat cheese salads

SERVES 4

Spinach Salad with Duck and Pears

(Salade Campagnarde aux Canard)

1 pound baby spinach, washed

4 ounces red onion, julienned

4 ounces blue cheese, crumbled

4 ounces walnuts, toasted

8–12 ounces shredded duck confit (or substitute cooked bacon or roasted pork)

2 d'Anjou, Bosc or Asian Pears, thinly sliced

4 ounces warm rendered duck fat or Fustini's Leccino EVOO

¼ cup Fustini's Wild Blueberry Balsamic

. . . .

Toss spinach with onions, blue cheese, walnuts, duck confit and pears.

Drizzle in duck fat or Fustini's Leccino EVOO and Fustini's Wild Blueberry Balsamic; toss again and serve.

Contributed by Blu, Glen Arbor

Jicama-Radish Salad
with Tangerine Vinaigrette

3 cups jicama, peeled, cut into 2-inch long julienne sticks

1 cup carrots, peeled, cut into 1-inch long matchstick strips

1 cup red radishes, cut into 1-inch long matchstick strips

12 large bibb lettuce, leaf lettuce or romaine leaves

¼ cup Fustini's Tangerine Balsamic

1 cup Fustini's Picholine EVOO

salt and pepper to taste

· ·

Peel and inspect jicama for firm texture, sweet taste and bright white color. Using a mandolin sharp French knife, carefully julienne.

Run peeled carrots and washed radishes through the fine blade of the mandolin or carefully cut into matchstick strips.

Combine ingredients in a large salad bowl.

To make vinaigrette, place Fustini's Tangerine Balsamic in a bowl and slowly add Fustini's Picholine EVOO as you whisk to emulsify. Add salt and pepper to taste.

When ready to serve, line 6 salad bowls with lettuce leaves. Toss salad with 1–2 tablespoons of dressing per serving and place atop leaves.

Contributed by Amical, Traverse City

SERVES 6

Shaved Fennel and Citrus Salad
with Ginger-Honey Vinaigrette

1 fennel bulb

2 fresh oranges

2 fresh ruby-red grapefruits

4 tablespoons pine nuts

1 cup baby spinach leaves

½ cup Ginger-Honey Vinaigrette (recipe follows)

. . . .

Clean fennel bulbs, trim fronds (set aside some for garnish) and shave paper thin with a mandoline or sharp knife, starting from the trimmed end and finishing at the root end.

Peel oranges, then remove outer white pith thoroughly and cut between membranes into supremes. Repeat with the grapefruit. Set aside.

Note: if preparing in advance, soak shaved fennel in cold water with a squeeze of lemon; thoroughly drain and pat dry prior to serving

Toast pine nuts in a dry skillet for a minute or two over medium heat, stirring or tossing constantly and being careful not to burn.

Toss shaved fennel and fruit with Ginger-Honey Vinaigrette (recipe follows). Place salad over a few baby spinach leaves and garnish with pine nuts and fennel fronds.

Continued...

Ginger-Honey Vinaigrette:

MAKES 2 CUPS

½ cup Fustini's Ginger and Honey Balsamic

1 tablespoon shallots, minced

1 tablespoon Dijon mustard

1 cup Fustini's Sweet Hojiblanca EVOO

¼ cup scallions, thinly sliced

1 teaspoon salt

dash white pepper

dash cayenne pepper

....

Place Fustini's Ginger and Honey Balsamic, shallots and mustard in a bowl. Blend with a handheld blender or whisk. Slowly add Fustini's Sweet Hojiblanca EVOO, continuing to blend or whisk until dressing has emulsified. Add scallions and season with salt and pepper.

Adapted from a recipe contributed by Amical, Traverse City

Peach and Cucumber Salad
with Peach-Garlic Vinaigrette

SERVES 4

1 large hothouse cucumber, unpeeled, sliced ¼-inch thick

½ cup Fustini's Peach Balsamic

½ teaspoon salt

¼ cup Fustini's Garlic EVOO

1 large tomato, seeded and coarsely chopped

1 pint blueberries

4 cups arugula

. . . .

Marinate cucumber slices in ¼ cup of Fustini's Peach Balsamic and salt in a large bowl for 30 minutes. Remove cucumber and whisk Fustini's Garlic EVOO slowly into balsamic until emulsified.

Add cucumbers back into bowl along with the tomato, blueberries and arugula and toss to combine.

Adapted from a recipe contributed by Fustini's of Traverse City

GREAT IDEAS:
- Marinate sliced cucumbers and top with sea salt and freshly ground pepper
- Combine with Basil or Meyer Lemon EVOO for a great salad dressing
- Combine with Garlic, Tunisian Harissa or Chipotle EVOO to marinate pork tenderloin or chicken
- Add to bottled water or sparkling mineral water for a refreshing thirst quencher

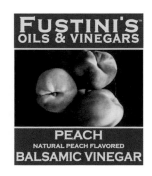

Tricolor Salad with Maytag Blue Cheese and Pear Vinaigrette

SERVES 4

2 heads Belgian endive, sliced on diagonal ¼-inch thick

½ head radicchio, torn into bite-sized pieces

2 cups arugula

2 tablespoons Fustini's Cinnamon Pear Balsamic

3 tablespoons Fustini's Roasted French Walnut Oil

1 lemon, juice only, divided

½ teaspoon salt

pepper to taste

½ cup Maytag blue cheese, crumbled

¾ cup candied walnuts (available in produce sections of many grocery stores)

. . . .

Place cut endive in a bowl of ice water with the juice of half a lemon to keep from turning brown. Toss radicchio and arugula together in a large bowl.

To make pear vinaigrette, place Fustini's Cinnamon Pear Balsamic in a bowl and slowly add Fustini's Roasted French Walnut Oil as you whisk to emulsify. Add juice of half a lemon, season with salt and pepper and whisk again.

Drain and dry endive and mix with radicchio and arugula. Toss lightly with vinaigrette, sprinkle with blue cheese, and dot with candied walnuts.

Adapted from a recipe contributed by Aerie, Traverse City

Winter Panzanella Salad

SERVES 6

2 bunches beets (gold and red), peeled and diced

3 shallots, sliced lengthwise

1 tablespoon mixed herbs of your choice, chopped

¼ cup Fustini's Picual EVOO, plus 2 tablespoons, divided

4 slices pancetta, small dice

1 loaf Italian bread, cut into large croutons

¼ cup honey

½ lemon, juice only

½ orange, juice only

2 tablespoons Fustini's Black Currant Balsamic

4 tablespoons Fustini's Meyer Lemon EVOO

salt and pepper to taste

1 handful dates, chopped

1 large handful arugula (or spinach)

1 log chevre (goat cheese)

....

Preheat oven to 350 degrees.

Toss beets with shallots and herbs in ¼ cup Fustini's Picual EVOO. Place in roasting pan and roast 20–30 minutes, or until beginning to caramelize.

Toss bread cubes in 2 tablespoons Fustini's Picual EVOO and bake in same oven 25–30 minutes to create croutons.

Meanwhile, cook pancetta in sauté pan and set aside.

Continued...

In a large salad bowl, mix honey, lemon juice, orange juice and Fustini's Black Currant Balsamic. Slowly whisk in Fustini's Meyer Lemon EVOO to emulsify. Add salt and pepper to taste.

Toss beets, shallots, pancetta, croutons, dates and arugula with dressing in bowl. Gently toss to coat. Top with crumbled chevre.

Contributed by Hanna Bistro, Traverse City

GREAT IDEAS:
- Brush on whitefish or other fish before baking, sautéing or grilling
- Combine with any Fustini's balsamic for a salad dressing. Particularly interesting with Red Apple Balsamic to dress a Waldorf Salad
- Drizzle on oatmeal or brush on toast
- Use in pesto instead of pine nuts
- Use as a substitute for other oils or butter in baking
- Combine with Cinnamon Pear Balsamic to roast sweet potatoes

GREAT IDEAS:
- Combine with Chipotle or Tunisian Harissa EVOO to marinate lamb, beef, pork or chicken when grilling
- Brush on pears, peaches, and pineapple prior to grilling for great caramelization
- Combine with Blood Orange or Persian Lime EVOO for salad dressing
- Drizzle on ice cream and fresh berries

MEATS, POULTRY & FISH

Pork Tenderloin Medallions with Fresh Cherry Salsa

SERVES 6

2 pork tenderloins (about 2 pounds)

½ cup fresh cilantro, chopped

½ cup shallots, chopped

1 cup Fustini's Cherry Balsamic

¼ cup Fustini's Persian Lime EVOO

salt and pepper to taste

Combine tenderloins with the next 4 ingredients in a large ziplock bag. Marinate 1 hour at room temperature or overnight in refrigerator.

When ready to cook, remove tenderloins from marinade and season with salt and pepper. Heat grill to medium high. Grill tenderloins about 15 minutes, turning at regular intervals so scoring occurs on all sides, until internal temperature registers 145 degrees.

Let tenderloins rest about 10 minutes, then slice ½-inch thick and serve with Fresh Cherry Salsa (recipe follows).

Fresh Cherry Salsa:

½ pound fresh dark cherries, pitted and halved

1 small jalapeño pepper, seeded, ribs removed and minced

½ cup fresh cilantro, chopped

2 tablespoons Fustini's Cherry Balsamic

2 tablespoons Fustini's Persian Lime EVOO

salt and pepper to taste

Combine all ingredients in a medium bowl, season with salt and pepper, and set aside to meld flavors.

Garlic-Peach Marinated Pork Tenderloin

SERVES 6

¼ cup Fustini's Peach Balsamic

2 tablespoons honey

1 teaspoon soy sauce

¼ teaspoon grated fresh ginger

¼ cup Fustini's Garlic EVOO

2 pork tenderloins

} or substitute 12 skin-on, bone-in chicken thighs

To make marinade, combine Fustini's Peach Balsamic with honey, soy sauce, ginger and Fustini's Garlic EVOO. Place pork or chicken in a large ziplock bag, pour marinade over, press air out, and refrigerate 4–12 hours.

When ready to cook, preheat oven to 350 degrees.

Remove meat from marinade, place on shallow baking sheet, and roast about 30 minutes or until thermometer registers 145 degrees for pork or 165 degrees for chicken. Meat may also be grilled.

Adapted from a recipe contributed by Hanna Bistro, Traverse City

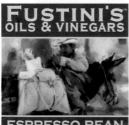

GREAT IDEAS:
- Combine with Tunisian Harissa or Chipotle EVOO and Garlic EVOO to marinate flank or skirt steaks; makes great fajitas
- Add to chili or baked beans as your "secret ingredient"
- Drizzle on fresh berries or ice cream
- For a great dessert, caramelize fresh pineapple chunks or brush on pears, peaches or pineapple rings, then grill
- Combine with Blood Orange EVOO for a pork tenderloin marinade

Barbecued Pork Ribs or Chicken

SERVES 4 – 6

2 pounds pork ribs (spareribs, country style or baby back)
or 2 pounds chicken (breasts, thighs, legs or wings)

2 12-ounce bottles dark beer

1 tablespoon liquid smoke

1 cup Fustini's Cinnamon Pear Balsamic

1 cup chili sauce

1 teaspoon chili powder (or cayenne pepper if you want a hotter sauce)

1 teaspoon finely chopped or pressed garlic

[or substitute Fustini's Chocolate or Espresso Bean Balsamic

Place ribs or chicken in large, non-metallic container, cover and marinate in beer and liquid smoke overnight.

To make barbecue sauce, combine Fustini's Cinnamon Pear Balsamic, chili sauce, chili powder and garlic in a saucepan. Simmer to reduce contents to desired consistency, approximately 15 minutes. Can be made a day ahead.

Preheat oven or grill to 325 degrees.

Bake or grill the ribs or chicken without sauce approximately 1 hour. Then baste with sauce and continue to bake or grill. For ribs, continue basting with sauce every 15 minutes until done (approximately 1 hour longer); internal temperature should register 160 degrees. For chicken, baste with sauce every 10 minutes until done (approximately 45 minutes longer); internal temperature should register 165 degrees.

Contributed by Fustini's of Ann Arbor

Chicken with Mushrooms and Sundried Tomatoes

SERVES 4

3 tablespoons Fustini's Basil EVOO, divided

4 skinless, boneless chicken breasts

1 shallot, finely chopped

8 ounces fresh mushrooms, thinly sliced

¼ cup sun-dried tomatoes (not oil packed), thinly sliced

1 tablespoon Fustini's 12 Year White Balsamic

3 tablespoons fresh basil, chiffonade, divided

½ cup heavy cream

¼ cup shredded Parmigiano Reggiano

. . . .

Heat 2 tablespoons Fustini's Basil EVOO in a skillet over medium heat. Add chicken and cook 10 minutes or until well browned on both sides. Remove chicken from pan.

Heat remaining 1 tablespoon Fustini's Basil EVOO in same pan over medium heat. Add shallots and cook, stirring continually, for 2 minutes. Stir in tomatoes, Fustini's 12 Year White Balsamic and 2 tablespoons basil.

Return chicken to skillet and bring liquid to a boil. Reduce heat to low. Simmer 5-10 minutes or until chicken is cooked through. Add cream and heat without boiling. Serve chicken and sauce with wide noodles and garnish with Parmigiano Reggiano and remaining 1 tablespoon basil.

Contributed by Fustini's of Petoskey

Chipotle-Marinated Chicken

SERVES 6

1 cup Fustini's Chipotle EVOO

4 tablespoons garlic, chopped

¾ cup cilantro leaves, coarsely chopped

2 tablespoons ground chili powder

salt and pepper to taste

1 roasting chicken, about 3½–4 pounds

....

To make marinade, whisk first 4 ingredients together. Add salt and pepper to taste. Refrigerate until needed.

Wash and dry chicken. Thoroughly rub whole bird with chipotle marinade, cover, and put in refrigerator for at least 8 hours or overnight.

When ready to roast, remove chicken from refrigerator. Preheat oven to 375 degrees. Roast 1½ to 1¾ hours, or until internal temperature registers 165 degrees.

Adapted from a recipe contributed by Amical, Traverse City

GREAT IDEAS:
- Brush on any fish before baking or grilling
- Drizzle over chopped fresh tomatoes for bruschetta and top with 18 Year Traditional Balsamic
- Combine with Strawberry, Raspberry or Lavender Balsamic for salad dressings
- Brush on bread for a grilled Caprese salad sandwich

FUSTINI'S OILS & VINEGARS

BASIL
NATURAL BASIL FLAVORED
EXTRA VIRGIN OLIVE OIL

Tequila-Lime Chicken

SERVES 4

2 limes, juice only

½ bunch fresh cilantro, roughly chopped

2 cloves fresh garlic, minced

¼ cup tequila

1 teaspoon cumin

1 jalapeño pepper, finely chopped

4 tablespoons Fustini's Chipotle EVOO or Cilantro and Onion EVOO, divided

4 boneless chicken breasts

salt and pepper to taste

. . . .

To make marinade, combine first 7 ingredients, up to and including 2 tablespoons Fustini's Chipotle EVOO, in a heavy-duty ziplock bag. Rinse chicken, pat dry, and place in bag with marinade. Refrigerate several hours or overnight.

Drain chicken and discard marinade. Grill or pan sauté chicken in 2 tablespoons Fustini's Chipotle EVOO on both sides in a skillet until nicely browned and cooked through, about 15 minutes or until internal temperature reads 165 degrees. Season to taste with salt and pepper. Slice each chicken breast on diagonal into 4–5 pieces.

Serve with Black Bean, Corn and Tomato salad (recipe page 40).

Chicken Hemingway
with Truffled Mushrooms

12 baby bella mushrooms, halved

4 tablespoons Fustini's Arbequina EVOO, divided

4 teaspoons Fustini's White Truffle EVOO

4 6-ounce boneless chicken breasts

¼ cup flour

2 eggs, beaten

1 cup panko bread crumbs

¼ cup diced onions

⅔ cup white wine

4 ounces chicken stock

½ cup heavy cream

4 tablespoons Fustini's Cherry Balsamic

dash of white pepper

2 tablespoons dried cherries

8 basil leaves, chiffonade

Sauté mushrooms in 1 tablespoon Fustini's Arbequina EVOO 5 minutes. Remove from pan and cool; place in a ziplock bag with Fustini's White Truffle Oil and marinate 30 minutes.

While mushrooms are marinating, coat chicken breasts in flour, then egg, and finally bread crumbs, covering evenly. Sauté in 2 tablespoons Fustini's Arbequina EVOO over medium-high heat for about 4 minutes per side or until internal temperature registers 165 degrees. Set aside and keep warm.

To make sauce, lightly sauté onion in 1 tablespoon Arbequina EVOO; strain out onion, reserving cooking liquid. Place liquid back into pan and add wine and stock. Bring to a boil; reduce heat and simmer until reduced by half. Add cream, Fustini's Cherry Balsamic, white pepper and cherries. Simmer over low heat about 5 minutes.

To serve, place one chicken breast on each of 4 plates. Divide sauce over chicken. Garnish with basil chiffonade and truffled mushrooms.

Adapted from a recipe contributed by the Terrace Inn, Bay View

GREAT IDEAS:
- Use to marinate lamb, beef, pork roasts and chops for a caramelized surface
- Combine with Sage and Wild Mushroom EVOO to marinate chicken or pork
- Combine with Meyer Lemon EVOO for salad dressing
- Drizzle on a Caprese salad or bruschetta
- Drizzle on ice cream with fresh berries

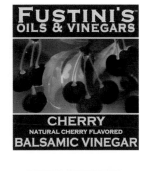

GREAT IDEAS:
- Combine with any Fustini's balsamic for salad dressings or roasting/grilling/sautéing vegetables
- Use in place of other oils for baking
- Great for bread dipping

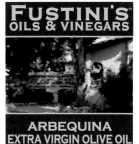

Grilled Steak and Vegetable Skewers

MAKES 4 SKEWERS

2 pounds top sirloin, cut into 16 1-inch pieces

8 mushrooms, halved

12 cherry tomatoes

½ cup Fustini's Leccino EVOO

½ teaspoon salt

¼ teaspoon pepper

⅓ cup packed brown sugar

3 tablespoons Fustini's Tangerine Balsamic

2 teaspoons Fustini's Roasted Sesame Oil

¼ cup sesame seeds

Soak 4 long wooden skewers in water 30 minutes (or use metal skewers). Preheat grill to high. Place meat, mushrooms and tomatoes in a large bowl. Add Fustini's Leccino EVOO and salt and pepper and toss to coat. Marinate about 30 minutes at room temperature.

Thread meat and vegetables onto skewers, alternating ingredients. Lay skewers on grill with handle ends facing out. If using wooden skewers, cover handle end with foil to prevent burning.

To make glaze, mix brown sugar, Fustini's Tangerine Balsamic and Fustini's Roasted Sesame Oil in a small bowl, stirring until sugar has dissolved.

Grill skewers, turning a few times, until meat begins to brown, about 3 minutes. Brush liberally with glaze and continue grilling until beef is lightly charred, 2–3 minutes longer. Transfer to a platter and sprinkle with sesame seeds.

Contributed by Fustini's of Holland

Sirloin Fiorentina with Sautéed Spinach

3 pounds top sirloin

3 tablespoons mixed fresh herbs (e.g., oregano, rosemary, thyme), chopped

2 tablespoons salt, divided

2 tablespoons pepper, divided

½ cup Fustini's Garlic EVOO, divided

4 pounds fresh spinach, washed and dried

1–2 tablespoons Fustini's Sicilian Lemon Balsamic

Heat grill to high. Brush sirloin with about ¼ cup Fustini's Garlic EVOO. Rub in 1 tablespoon salt, 1 tablespoon pepper and fresh herbs. Grill steaks to desired doneness, 120–125 degrees for rare, 140–145 degrees for medium. Cover and let rest 10 minutes.

Meanwhile, wash spinach and drain, leaving some moisture on the leaves. Coat a large skillet with remaining Fustini's Garlic EVOO and heat to medium. Add spinach and cook just enough to wilt. Drizzle with Fustini's Sicilian Lemon Balsamic at time of serving. Season with remaining salt and pepper to taste.

Slice sirloin across grain into ¼-inch strips and serve over spinach and Truffled Grits with Goat Cheese (recipe page 85).

Adapted from a recipe contributed by Hanna Bistro, Traverse City

GREAT IDEAS:
- Combine with any Fustini's balsamic to marinate or grill chicken or seafood
- Drizzle on rice or pasta or add to oriental rice or noodle soup
- Combine with Basil EVOO to roast or sauté vegetables
- Use as finishing oil for Asian recipes

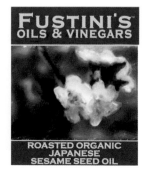

Seared Tuna with Pineapple-Mango Salsa

SERVES 4

Pineapple-Mango Salsa:

1 cup pineapple, finely chopped

1 ripe mango, peeled, pitted and diced

½ medium red onion, finely chopped

1 jalapeño pepper, ribs and seeds removed, minced (include seeds if you want it hot)

1 small cucumber, diced

½ red bell pepper, diced

3 tablespoons fresh cilantro, chopped

3 tablespoons Fustini's Persian Lime EVOO

3 tablespoons Fustini's Mango Balsamic (or substitute Fustini's Golden Pineapple Balsamic)

1 lime, juice only

· ·

Mix all ingredients together and set aside. May also be prepared several hours ahead; refrigerate and bring to room temperature before serving.

Tuna:

1 teaspoon ground cumin	¼ teaspoon pepper
1 teaspoon ground coriander	4 6-ounce sushi-grade tuna steaks
1 tablespoon salt	Fustini's Manzanillo EVOO

· ·

Mix spices together with salt and pepper; rub into tuna steaks. Heat Fustini's Manzanillo EVOO until it just begins to smoke. Sear tuna steaks for about 2–3 minutes per side, until medium rare (about 125 degrees internal temperature). Serve with Pineapple-Mango Salsa.

Adapted from a recipe contributed by Fustini's of Holland

Smoked Paprika Salmon with Orzo and Arugula Salad

SERVES 4

1¼ cups Fustini's Asian Blackberry Balsamic, divided

4 salmon fillets

¼ cup Fustini's Persian Lime EVOO

2 tablespoons smoked paprika

salt and pepper to taste

4 tablespoons butter

2 cups orzo pasta, cooked al dente

½ cup fresh mozzarella, diced

2 cups arugula

½ cup cherry tomatoes, halved

3 tablespoons Fustini's Blood Orange EVOO

4 lemon slices

....

Make reduction of 1 cup Fustini's Asian Blackberry Balsamic. Set aside.

Heat grill to medium hot. Brush salmon fillets with Fustini's Persian Lime EVOO; dust with smoked paprika, salt and pepper. Grill to desired doneness. While fish is grilling, melt butter in a sauté pan, add orzo pasta, and reheat slowly.

To make arugula salad, place mozzarella in a small mixing bowl and season lightly with salt and pepper. Add arugula and tomatoes and toss with Fustini's Blood Orange EVOO and ¼ cup Fustini's Asian Blackberry Balsamic.

Drizzle salmon with a little Fustini's Asian Blackberry Balsamic reduction and serve with orzo pasta and arugula salad. Garnish with lemon slices.

Adapted from a recipe contributed by 84 East Food & Spirits, Holland

Herb-Roasted Smallmouth Bass

SERVES 4

1 whole smallmouth bass (about 3 pounds), eviscerated and scaled, head and tail intact

¼ cup Fustini's Tarragon EVOO

2 cups of mixed fresh herbs (e.g., tarragon, Italian parsley, thyme, rosemary, cilantro), finely chopped, plus sprigs for garnish

2 garlic cloves, minced

salt and pepper to taste

1 lemon, cut into wedges

Note: If bass is not available, red snapper is a good substitute

Preheat oven to 500 degrees (or 450 degrees convection).

Wash and dry fish thoroughly. Cut three long diagonal slits in each side. Sprinkle lightly with salt and pepper inside and out, including insides of slits. Make a paste of Fustini's Tarragon EVOO, chopped herbs, garlic and salt and pepper. Rub paste all over fish, pushing some into slits.

Roast fish on a lightly oiled, rimmed baking sheet for 20 minutes, until skin is brown and crispy and flesh flakes easily but is still moist. Internal temperature should register about 140 degrees. Let rest for 5–10 minutes.

To serve, remove head, tail and skin and separate fillet from one side of backbone. Lift backbone from bottom fillet. Remove as many remaining bones as possible. Serve with lemon wedges.

POTATOES, PASTAS & GRAINS

Baby Yukon Gold Potato Salad
with Crispy Pancetta

SERVES 6 – 8

4 pounds baby Yukon Gold potatoes, peeled and cut into ¼-inch slices

5 cups chicken broth

¼ cup Fustini's Provençal Herbes EVOO

6 ounces pancetta, sliced ⅛-inch thick and chopped

1 cup celery, sliced thinly

½ cup onion, diced finely

2 cups scallions greens, sliced thinly

2 tablespoons Fustini's White Truffle EVOO

2 tablespoons fresh lemon juice

Boil potatoes in chicken broth until just tender; drain, reserving broth, and set aside.

Return broth to pan and reduce until just ⅔ cup remains. Pour over potatoes and toss gently.

Heat Fustini's Provençal Herbes EVOO in a large skillet; add pancetta and sauté until crisp.

Mix pancetta, celery, onion and scallion greens with potatoes. Fold in Fustini's White Truffle EVOO and lemon juice. Serve chilled or at room temperature.

Adapted from a recipe by Roast and Toast, Petoskey

Roasted Potatoes
with Red Peppers and Onions

SERVES 4

4 cups red potatoes, quartered

2 tablespoons Fustini's Chipotle EVOO

2 tablespoons Fustini's 18 Year Traditional Balsamic

1 red bell pepper, thinly sliced

½ red onion, thinly sliced

salt to taste

Preheat oven to 350 degrees.

Toss potatoes in Fustini's Chipotle EVOO and sprinkle with salt. Roast on a rimmed sheet pan approximately 25–30 minutes or until browned.

Slowly heat Fustini's 18 Year Traditional Balsamic in a large skillet. Add peppers and onions to pan and stir until caramelized (just a few minutes, or longer if you like your veggies a bit more cooked—you might have to add a bit more balsamic if you cook them longer).

Add peppers and onions to the potatoes, then sprinkle with salt and serve.

Contributed by Fustini's of Traverse City

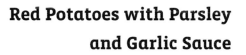

Red Potatoes with Parsley and Garlic Sauce

SERVES 4 – 6

1½ pounds small red potatoes

1 tablespoon Fustini's Tuscan Herb EVOO

1 medium onion, chopped

2 garlic cloves, finely chopped

1 cup chicken broth

1 cup fresh parsley, chopped

½ teaspoon pepper

Peel a strip of skin from around middle of each potato and place potatoes in a bowl of cold water (discard potato skin strips).

Heat Fustini's Tuscan Herb EVOO; sauté onion and garlic for 5 minutes. Add broth and ¾ cup parsley. Mix well and bring to a boil.

Place potatoes in broth and return to a boil. Reduce heat and simmer 10 minutes. Remove potatoes to a bowl with slotted spoon. Add pepper to skillet and stir. Pour broth over potatoes and sprinkle with remaining parsley.

Contributed by Fustini's of Holland

GREAT IDEAS:
- Great for sautéing, roasting or grilling vegetables, beef, pork, lamb, poultry or fish
- Drizzle on pasta and mix in prosciutto and caramelized red onions
- Combine with Lavender, 12 Year Traditional or 18 Year Traditional Balsamic for an excellent dressing
- Mix with grated Parmigiano Reggiano and 18 Year Traditional Balsamic for bread dipping
- Great alone for bread dipping

Bucatini with Italian Sausage, Peppers and Onions

SERVES 6 – 8

¼ cup Fustini's Tuscan Herb EVOO, divided

1 large sweet onion, sliced thinly on the bias

6 large garlic cloves, sliced thinly

1½ pounds hot Italian sausage

3 Ancient Sweets long peppers (or other sweet red pepper), seeded, ribs removed, sliced thinly

8 ounces white or brown mushrooms, quartered

½–1 teaspoon dried hot chili flakes

1 tablespoon fennel seeds, crushed with a mortar and pestle

2 14½-ounce cans crushed tomatoes

1 tablespoon plus 1 teaspoon salt, divided

1 teaspoon freshly ground black pepper

3 tablespoons fresh Italian parsley, oregano, basil or other herbs, coarsely chopped

1 tablespoon Fustini's 12 Year Traditional Balsamic

½ cup Pecorino Romano, grated

½ cup Parmigiano Reggiano, grated

1 pound bucatini (or substitute spaghetti or penne)

fresh basil sprigs for garnish

. . . .

Heat ⅛ cup Fustini's Tuscan Herb EVOO in a large stockpot and sauté onions and garlic about 3 minutes. Add Italian sausage and cook over medium heat until no longer pink, breaking up sausage with a spoon. Add peppers, mushrooms, dried hot chili flakes and fennel seeds to pot and cook 5 minutes. Add tomatoes and 1 teaspoon salt. Bring to a boil, then lower heat and simmer about 30 minutes, stirring occasionally. Stir in fresh herbs and Fustini's 12 Year Traditional Balsamic. Simmer an additional 10–15 minutes.

Continued...

Meanwhile, bring a large pot of water to a boil. Add 1 tablespoon salt. Cook bucatini according to package directions, usually about 10–12 minutes. Drain and reserve about ¼ cup cooking water, in case sauce needs to be thinned a bit.

Divide bucatini among warmed pasta bowls and spoon some of the sauce over. Sprinkle with a little of each of the cheeses and garnish with fresh basil sprigs.

GREAT IDEAS:
- Drizzle on pasta
- Use to cook rice or risotto
- Combine with Tangerine Balsamic to marinate poultry and pork
- Combine with Lavender Balsamic to marinate beef and lamb
- Use to roast potatoes and vegetables
- Great for bread dipping
- Combine with any of the vinegars for a fresh-flavored green salad dressing

GREAT IDEAS:
- Combine with Chipotle or Tunisian Harissa EVOO for grilling
- Drizzle over steamed or roasted vegetables
- Drizzle on bruschetta or Caprese salad
- Drizzle over fruit or ice cream
- Combine with any Fustini's EVOO for bread dipping

GREAT IDEAS:
- Marinate cucumbers or water chestnuts in Ginger and Honey Balsamic and serve alone or add to salad
- Sear tuna or salmon in any Fustini's EVOO, then deglaze pan with Ginger and Honey Balsamic and drizzle glaze over fish
- Use in stir-fry dishes
- Flavor rice
- Great on fruit salads or green salads
- Add to bottled or sparkling water for refreshing flavor

Greek Pasta Salad with Garbanzo Beans

SERVES 6

½ pound tubular or other shaped pasta

1 16-ounce can garbanzo beans

1 16-ounce can artichoke hearts (not marinated)

1 small jar pitted Kalamata olives (about ½–¾ cup)

2 red bell peppers (or use jarred roasted peppers), sliced in thin strips

6 ounces feta cheese, crumbled

¼ cup Fustini's Garlic EVOO

¼ cup Fustini's Sicilian Lemon Balsamic

salt and pepper to taste

· ·

Cook pasta in boiling, salted water until al dente. Rinse under cold water.

Drain garbanzo beans. Drain and roughly chop artichoke hearts and Kalamata olives. Toss all ingredients together, up to and including feta, in large mixing bowl with Fustini's Garlic EVOO and Fustini's Sicilian Lemon Balsamic. Season to taste with salt and pepper.

Contributed by Fustini's of Traverse City

Sundried Tomato Linguine with Chicken and Broccoli

SERVES 4 – 6

1 pound sundried tomato linguine (or substitute regular linguine)

2 tablespoons Fustini's Oregano Balsamic, plus more to taste

6 tablespoons Fustini's Basil EVOO, divided, plus more to taste

2 pounds broccoli, cut into bite-sized florets

1 pound boneless chicken breast, cut into 1-inch pieces

1 cup oil-packed sundried tomatoes, halved

½ cup fresh basil leaves, julienned

1 cup Parmigiano Reggiano (or substitute Pecorino Romano)

salt to taste

. . . .

Cook pasta in 6–8 quarts of rapidly boiling, salted water until al dente (about 8–10 minutes). Drain and transfer to large, warmed bowl; toss with 2 tablespoons Fustini's Oregano Balsamic and 2 tablespoons Fustini's Basil EVOO.

Cook broccoli florets 2 minutes in just enough boiling water to cover; drain and set aside.

Heat remaining olive oil in large heavy skillet. Add chicken and cook until no longer pink. Add broccoli and sauté for 2 minutes, or until heated through.

Toss chicken and broccoli with pasta. Mix in tomatoes and basil, reserving some basil for garnish. Top with cheese. Drizzle on more EVOO and balsamic to taste. Garnish with julienned basil. Serve in warmed pasta bowls.

Adapted from a recipe contributed by Fustini's of Holland

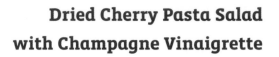

Dried Cherry Pasta Salad
with Champagne Vinaigrette

SERVES 6

1 pound bowtie pasta, cooked al dente

1 tablespoon Fustini's Leccino EVOO

8 ounces diced cubed cooked turkey

3 ounces dried cherries

½ cup medium diced yellow onion

½ cup medium diced celery

½ cup toasted whole almonds

Place all ingredients in a large bowl and toss with Champagne Vinaigrette (recipe follows).

Champagne Vinaigrette:

2 cups mayonnaise

2 tablespoons Dijon mustard

¼ cup confectioner's sugar

2 tablespoons Fustini's Champagne Vinegar

2 tablespoons water

½ teaspoon poppy seeds

½ teaspoon pepper

2 teaspoons salt

Whisk all ingredients together in a medium bowl.

Contributed by Fustini's of Holland

SERVES 4

Truffled Grits with Goat Cheese

1 quart half and half

½ cup white grits

1 tablespoon garlic, minced

½ teaspoon Tabasco (optional)

1 tablespoon unsalted butter

¼ cup goat cheese

½ tablespoon Fustini's White Truffle EVOO

1 teaspoon parsley, finely chopped

salt and pepper to taste

. . . .

In a large saucepan over medium-high heat, bring half and half, garlic and Tabasco (if using) to a slow, rolling boil. Reduce heat to low and whisk in grits. Continue whisking over very low heat until grits begin to thicken.

Add butter, goat cheese, Fustini's White Truffle EVOO and parsley.

Season to taste with salt and pepper.

Variation: Substitute 1–2 tablespoons Fustini's Porcini EVOO for Fustini's White Truffle EVOO.

Contributed by Hanna Bistro, Traverse City

Wild Mushroom Risotto with Truffle Oil

SERVES 6

1½ ounces dried porcini mushrooms

1 ounce dried chanterelles

5 cups hot water

1–2 32-ounce cartons chicken broth

3 tablespoons Fustini's Sage and Wild Mushroom EVOO

1 large yellow onion, chopped

8 ounces shitake or baby portabella mushrooms, cleaned and sliced

2½ cups Arborio or Carnaroli rice

1 cup (or more) dry white wine   Sauvignon Blanc or Pinot
                                     Grigio work well
1 teaspoon fresh thyme, chopped

⅓ cup half-and-half

½–1 cup freshly grated Parmigiano Reggiano

salt and freshly ground pepper to taste

1 tablespoon Fustini's White Truffle EVOO

Parmigiano Reggiano, shaved

In a medium bowl, soak dried mushrooms in hot water. Let stand 30 minutes to soften. With a slotted spoon, remove mushrooms from soaking liquid, reserving liquid. Chop mushrooms coarsely and set aside.

Strain soaking liquid through a cheesecloth-lined sieve into a medium saucepan. Add broth and bring to a simmer. Adjust heat to keep liquid hot but not boiling.

In a large, heavy saucepan or stockpot over medium heat, warm Fustini's Sage and Wild Mushroom EVOO. Add onion and sauté until it begins to soften and turns transparent, about 5 minutes. Add all of the mushrooms and stir until they begin to soften, about 5 minutes.

Continued...

Add rice and stir until white spots appear in the center of the grains, about 1 minute. Add wine and chopped thyme and stir until liquid is nearly absorbed, about 2–3 minutes. Add more broth a ladleful at a time, stirring frequently, until rice is al dente and mixture is creamy, 20–25 minutes longer.

Add half-and-half and grated Parmigiano Reggiano. Stir to mix well. Fold in Fustini's White Truffle EVOO.

Serve in warmed individual pasta bowls and garnish with shaved Parmigiano Reggiano.

GREAT IDEAS:
- Drizzle over noodles and smoked Gouda cheese
- Great for cooking omelets, frittatas, scrambled eggs
- Sauté dry rice in Sage and Wild Mushroom EVOO until translucent, add liquid, then cook as directed
- Use in place of butter for mashed potatoes
- Combine with Red Apple Balsamic to inject into and baste turkey

GREAT IDEAS:
- A finishing oil on steaks and potatoes, eggs and rice dishes
- Mix with Sicilian Lemon or Tangerine Balsamic for a delicious salad dressing

Orzo Market Salad

SERVES 4 – 6

2 boneless chicken breasts, trimmed of fat and tendons

¼ cup Fustini's Arbequina EVOO, for brushing

2 cups orzo, uncooked

3 ears fresh corn (about 2½ cups)

1 cup cherry tomatoes, halved

1 8-ounce block feta cheese, cut into medium dice

1 lemon, juice and zest

1 large bunch fresh basil, chiffonade

½ cup fresh chives, cut into small pieces with kitchen scissors

4 tablespoons Fustini's Basil EVOO

salt and pepper to taste

. . . .

Heat grill to medium-high. Brush chicken breasts with Fustini's Arbequina EVOO and grill about 10 minutes per side (20 minutes total), until internal temperature reads 165 degrees. When cool enough to handle, cut chicken into bite-sized pieces and chill.

Meanwhile, bring 3 cups of water to a boil. Add orzo. Reduce heat to medium and cook 5–7 minutes, until orzo is al dente. Drain and transfer to a large bowl to cool. Toss with fork a few times while cooling to prevent sticking.

Remove husks from corn and cut kernels off the cob. Cook in boiling salted water for 3 minutes. Rinse under cold running water and drain.

Toss chicken, orzo, corn, tomatoes and feta together. Add lemon juice and zest, basil, chives and Fustini's Basil EVOO. Season to taste with salt and pepper.

Contributed by Limonata, Holland

VEGETABLES

Rainbow Swiss Chard
with Tomatoes and Red Onion

SERVES 4 – 6

3 tablespoons Fustini's Frantoio EVOO

1 red onion, halved and sliced on the bias

2 pounds rainbow Swiss chard

2 large or 6 small tomatoes, quartered

1–2 tablespoons Fustini's 18 Year Traditional Balsamic

salt and pepper to taste

. . . .

Trim stems and remove thick ribs from Swiss chard; cut stems into bite-sized pieces and chop leaves coarsely. Wash and dry thoroughly in a salad spinner. Set aside. Heat Fustini's Frantoio EVOO until hot, but not smoking, in a large skillet or pot with high sides. Add onions and Swiss chard stems. Sauté 5 minutes. Add greens a few handfuls at a time, stirring and making further additions as they wilt. Add tomatoes and stir. Cook about 10 minutes, until greens are soft and tomatoes have rendered some of their juice. Stir in Fustini's 18 Year Traditional Balsamic. Season to taste with salt and pepper.

GREAT IDEAS:
- Combine with Sicilian Lemon Balsamic, drizzle over pasta, top with grated Asiago cheese and chopped fresh Roma tomatoes, add freshly cracked black pepper and toss
- Use to sauté or grill vegetables
- Combine with Pinot Noir Wine Vinegar, Dijon mustard, fresh garlic and basil for a great vinaigrette dressing

Baby Spinach and Roasted Red Pepper Sauté

SERVES 4

1 tablespoon garlic, minced

½ tablespoon shallots, minced

4 cups baby spinach

½ cup roasted red pepper, julienned

2 tablespoons Fustini's Meyer Lemon EVOO

salt and pepper to taste

Variation: Substitute arugula for baby spinach

Place garlic and shallots in a skillet with 1 tablespoon Fustini's Meyer Lemon EVOO. Over medium-low heat, sauté until lightly browned. Add baby spinach and roasted red pepper. Cook until spinach is just slightly wilted. Season to taste with salt and pepper. Drizzle remaining 1 tablespoon Fustini's Meyer Lemon EVOO over spinach to serve.

Contributed by Hanna Bistro, Traverse City

SERVES 8 – 10

Sauce:

⅓ cup Fustini's Basil EVOO, plus more for frying

2 garlic cloves, minced

1 cup black olives, pitted and halved

2 28-ounce cans crushed tomatoes

⅓ cup Fustini's Oregano Balsamic

¼ cup fresh basil leaves, torn into small pieces

salt and pepper to taste

. . . .

Heat Fustini's Basil EVOO in a large saucepan; add garlic and cook 1 minute. Add olives and cook 2 minutes, stirring often. Stir in tomatoes with juices and bring to a low simmer. Stir in Fustini's Oregano Balsamic and basil and season with salt and pepper. Simmer 10 minutes. Remove from heat and set aside.

Cheese Filling:

2 pounds ricotta cheese

1¼ cups Parmigiano Reggiano, grated, divided

2 eggs

½ cup fresh basil leaves, chopped

salt and pepper to taste

2 pounds mozzarella, shredded

. . . .

Stir together ricotta and ½ cup Parmigiano Reggiano, reserving remaining ¾ cup Parmigiano for later. Mix in eggs and basil and season with salt and pepper. Reserve shredded mozzarella for later. Set aside.

Continued...

Eggplant:

4 cups panko bread crumbs

1 tablespoon garlic powder

1 tablespoon dried oregano

Salt and pepper, to taste

3 eggs

1 cup flour

½ –1 cup Fustini's Basil EVOO, plus more for oiling baking dish

3 medium-large eggplants, cut lengthwise into ½-inch-thick slices

. . . .

Preheat oven to 350 degrees.

Combine panko, garlic powder and oregano in a shallow bowl; season generously with salt and pepper and mix well. Break eggs into another shallow bowl; season with salt and pepper and beat with a fork to mix. Put flour in another shallow bowl and season with salt and pepper. Arrange eggplant, flour, eggs and panko on a work surface near stovetop.

Dredge several eggplant slices in flour, then dip in egg, and finally coat in panko. Heat about ½ cup olive oil in a large skillet until hot but not smoking. Arrange eggplant in a single layer in skillet and cook until tender and well browned on both sides. Do not crowd, or eggplant will not brown. Drain on paper towels. Repeat with remaining eggplant, adding more olive oil to skillet as needed.

Rub a large glass or oven-safe ceramic baking dish with Fustini's Basil EVOO. Spread some of the sauce over bottom of dish. Add a layer of eggplant. Spread with half of the ricotta mixture. Add another layer of tomato sauce and sprinkle with about ⅓ of the mozzarella. Repeat with a layer of eggplant, remaining ricotta, tomato sauce, and another ⅓ of the mozzarella. Finish with remaining eggplant, remaining tomato sauce, and remaining mozzarella. Sprinkle with reserved ¾ cup Parmigiano Reggiano. Bake approximately 1 hour, until golden and bubbling. Let stand about 20 minutes before cutting.

Italian Green Beans with Garlic

SERVES 4

1 pound Italian green beans, stem ends trimmed

3 garlic cloves, sliced thinly

2 tablespoons Fustini's Garlic EVOO

1 teaspoon Fustini's 12 Year White Balsamic

salt and pepper to taste

fresh Italian parsley, finely chopped

Cook green beans in boiling, salted water about 5 minutes. Drain well. Meanwhile, sauté garlic in Fustini's Garlic EVOO in a skillet over medium-low heat 4–5 minutes, being careful not to burn. Remove garlic and reserve. Add green beans to pan and increase heat to medium-high. Sauté until they begin to take on a little color.

Return garlic to pan and add Fustini's 12 Year White Balsamic. Bring to a boil. Pour beans, garlic and sauce into a warmed plate and season to taste with salt and pepper. Garnish with fresh parsley.

Grilled Romaine
with Lemon-Parmesan Vinaigrette

SERVES 6

Lemon-Parmesan Vinaigrette:

¼ cup Fustini's Meyer Lemon EVOO

1 teaspoon lemon zest

2 tablespoons lemon juice

2 cloves garlic, minced

2 teaspoons Dijon mustard

1 teaspoon Worcestershire sauce

¼ cup Parmigiano Reggiano, grated

pepper to taste

Whisk together the Fustini's Meyer Lemon EVOO, lemon zest and juice, garlic, mustard and Worcestershire sauce. Stir in cheese and pepper.

Grilled Romaine:

3 hearts of romaine lettuce

Fustini's Meyer Lemon EVOO, for brushing

Parmigiano Reggiano, shaved into shards using a potato peeler

Preheat grill over medium-high heat. Lightly oil grill surface. Remove any wilted outer leaves from romaine heads, then cut each one in half, lengthwise, leaving the root end intact so that each half holds together. Brush lightly with Fustini's Meyer Lemon EVOO. Grill lettuce, cut side down, until grill marks form and lettuce just starts to wilt, about 5 minutes, turning once. Serve drizzled with Lemon-Parmesan Vinaigrette and garnish with shaved Parmigiano Reggiano.

Baby Carrots with Ginger, Honey and Lemon Glaze

SERVES 4

¼ cup Fustini's Sicilian Lemon Balsamic

¾ cup Fustini's Ginger and Honey Balsamic

3 tablespoons cold butter

1 pound fresh baby carrots with greens

1 teaspoon salt

¼ cup fresh parsley, finely chopped

Cut all but 1 inch of carrot greens away and discard. Scrub carrots with a vegetable brush, but do not peel.

To make glaze, combine balsamics in a small pan and reduce by half over medium heat, stirring occasionally and watching to make sure the mixture doesn't burn. Stir in cold butter and keep glaze warm.

Meanwhile, bring about ½ inch of water and salt to a boil in a large skillet. Add carrots, reduce heat to a simmer, and cook 6–7 minutes.

Pour glaze over carrots and combine gently. Garnish with parsley.

GREAT IDEAS:
- Combine with Basil or Garlic EVOO for a great marinade for vegetables and seafoods
- Combine with Basil EVOO and drizzle over fresh pasta
- Great on ice cream or fruit salad or in sparkling water

Braised Cabbage and Apples

SERVES 6 – 8

2 tablespoons unsalted butter

3 tablespoons Fustini's Barnea EVOO

1 onion, sliced thinly

½ red cabbage, julienned

½ green cabbage, julienned

2 tart red apples, peeled, cored and sliced

2 tablespoons Fustini's Cinnamon Pear Balsamic

2 tablespoons Fustini's Red Apple Balsamic

1 teaspoon salt

½ teaspoon pepper

2 tablespoons sugar

In a large saucepan or Dutch oven, heat butter and Fustini's Barnea EVOO over low heat; add onion and sauté about 5 minutes, or until soft. Add cabbage, apples, Fustini's Cinnamon Pear Balsamic and Fustini's Red Apple Balsamic and simmer about 30 minutes. Season with salt, pepper and sugar.

GREAT IDEAS:
- Combine with Blood Orange or Persian Lime EVOO for a salad dressing on spinach or arugula salad, then add fresh strawberries, Roasted French Walnut Oil, mandarin orange slices and feta cheese; or caramelize pears or apples and substitute goat cheese for feta
- Drizzle into yogurt, over ice cream or over apple crisp
- Use as a glaze on grilled salmon

Spaghetti Squash with Pomodoro Sauce

1 spaghetti squash (about 1½ pounds)

2 garlic cloves, minced

1 small onion, finely chopped

1 teaspoon Fustini's Garlic EVOO

1 teaspoon Fustini's Persian Lime EVOO

3 tablespoons tomato paste

½ pound fresh plum tomatoes, roughly chopped

1 teaspoon Fustini's Champagne Vinegar

1 teaspoon dried oregano

1 teaspoon dried basil

½ teaspoon red pepper flakes

fresh basil for garnish

. . . .

Preheat oven to 375 degrees.

Halve squash lengthwise and scoop out seeds. Coat a baking sheet with cooking spray; lay squash halves, flesh side down, on sheet. Bake 35 minutes or until shell can be easily pierced.

While squash bakes, sauté garlic and onion in Fustini's Garlic EVOO and Fustini's Persian Lime EVOO over medium heat 5 minutes. Add remaining ingredients (except fresh basil) and cook, stirring occasionally, 30 minutes. Lower heat if sauce begins to boil.

Remove squash from oven. Scrape crosswise to pull strands from shell. Place squash in nonmetal serving bowl. Pour sauce over and garnish with fresh basil.

Contributed by Fustini's of Petoskey

SERVES 4

Roasted Red and Golden Beets

2 pounds mixed small red and golden beets with greens

½ cup Fustini's Provençal Herbes EVOO

salt and pepper to taste

Fustini's 12 Year Traditional Balsamic for garnish

Preheat oven to 400 degrees.

Cut all but 1 inch of beet greens away and discard. Wash beets and dry with paper towels. Toss with Fustini's Provençal Herbes EVOO. Roast 1 hour or until still somewhat resistant when pierced with the tip of a sharp knife.

When cool enough to handle, rub off skins with a damp paper towel. Cut beets into ¼-inch-thick slices. Drizzle with Fustini's Provençal Herbes EVOO and dot with Fustini's 12 Year Traditional Balsamic.

GREAT IDEAS:
- Use a splash in soups and on seafood
- Combine with Garlic, Tuscan Herb or Provençal Herbes EVOO for a savory salad dressing
- Combine with Meyer Lemon, Persian Lime or Blood Orange EVOO for a tart citrus dressing on salads or for roasting asparagus, Brussels sprouts or green beans

DESSERTS

SERVES 8

Dough for Double-crust Pie (top and bottom crust):

4 cups all-purpose flour

1½ cups very cold vegetable shortening, pre-cut into 1-inch cubes

1 teaspoon salt

¾ cup very cold water

or substitute cold cubed butter for shortening

Combine flour, shortening and salt in a medium bowl and work together with pastry cutter until they form a coarse, crumbly mixture. Add water all at once in center of mixture and move through mixture with pastry cutter until dough is no longer crumbly in bottom of bowl. Do not go any further, as this will result in an overmixed, tough dough. Let dough stand for at least 1 hour at room temperature.

Separate dough into 2 equal-sized balls. With a floured rolling pin on a lightly floured surface, roll each ball into a 10-inch diameter round. Lay one round over a 9-inch pie pan and press dough into pan. Set the other round aside and use to top the pie after adding filling.

Continued...

FUSTINI'S
OILS & VINEGARS

RED APPLE
NATURAL RED APPLE FLAVORED
BALSAMIC VINEGAR

GREAT IDEAS:
- Combine with Sage and Wild Mushroom EVOO to baste and inject into turkey
- Drizzle on sweet potatoes and roast
- Drizzle on apple crisp
- Combine with Roasted French Walnut Oil, Garlic EVOO or Toasted Pumpkin Seed Oil for salad dressing
- Combine with Cilantro and Onion EVOO, then brush on acorn squash before baking

Pie Filling:

8–10 tart apples (such as Northern Spy or Granny Smith), cored, peeled and sliced

2 tablespoons Fustini's Cinnamon Pear Balsamic

¾ cup sugar

⅓ cup flour

½ teaspoon cinnamon

½ teaspoon salt

Optional garnish:

vanilla ice cream

½ cup Fustini's Red Apple Balsamic, reduced by half

....

Preheat oven to 350 degrees (or 325 degrees for convection).

Toss apples in Fustini's Cinnamon Pear Balsamic.

Combine sugar, flour, cinnamon and salt. Toss apples with this mixture in a bowl to evenly coat.

Pour fruit mixture into pie crust. Gently press apples into bottom of crust.

Place top crust over apples, then gently press edges of top crust into edges of bottom crust to seal the filling. To flute edges, press finger and thumb of one hand together and rest gently on the outer crust facing out, then with the index finger of your other hand press into the dough where your other hand rests. Repeat this at ½-inch intervals as you move around the perimeter of the pie, creating an attractive fluted edge along the outer crust.

Note: If you already have your own method for fluting, go ahead and do it your way

Place pie on a rimmed baking sheet lined with parchment paper or foil to catch drippings. Place in center of oven and bake 90 minutes. Keep an eye on the pie after 60 minutes; it will be done when crust is golden and filling is bubbling. Cool on a rack for one hour prior to slicing.

Serve with a scoop of vanilla ice cream, drizzled with a reduction of Fustini's Red Apple Balsamic, if desired.

Contributed by Grand Traverse Pie Company, Traverse City

SERVES 4

Roasted Pears with Cinnamon Pear Balsamic

4 Bosc pears

4 teaspoons Michigan maple syrup, divided

¾ cup Fustini's Cinnamon Pear Balsamic

vanilla ice cream or whipped cream for serving

1 cup fresh seasonal berries for garnish

fresh mint for garnish

. . . .

Preheat oven to 425 degrees.

Halve and core pears, leaving stems intact. Pour ½ inch of water into bottom of an 8 x 8-inch shallow baking dish. Place pears in dish and drizzle 1 teaspoon maple syrup into each hollowed-out center. Add remaining maple syrup around pears.

Bake for approximately 45 minutes or until tender and slightly browned.

Meanwhile, in a small, heavy-bottomed saucepan, reduce Fustini's Cinnamon Pear Balsamic by half; it should be the consistency of syrup.

Pour a small pool of balsamic reduction onto a dessert plate and place one warm roasted pear in center of plate. Serve with vanilla ice cream or whipped cream and garnish with berries and fresh mint.

Contributed by Julienne Tomatoes, Petoskey

Peach-Blueberry Cobbler

SERVES 6

Cobbler Filling:

4 tablespoons Fustini's Peach Balsamic

¾ cup sugar

10 firm, ripe freestone peaches, peeled and sliced

1 teaspoon ground cinnamon

1 pint fresh blueberries

4 tablespoons cornstarch slurry — 1 tablespoon cornstarch mixed with 3 tablespoons water

Crumble Topping (recipe follows)

Optional garnish:

vanilla ice cream

½ cup Fustini's Wild Blueberry Balsamic, reduced by half

. . . .

Preheat oven to 375 degrees (350 degrees for convection).

Place Fustini's Peach Balsamic in a saucepan over medium heat. Add sugar and stir to dissolve. Before mixture bubbles, add peaches and cinnamon. Toss to heat evenly, taking care that peaches do not lose their shape. Add cornstarch slurry and stir until thickened; remove from heat and cool. When cool, fold in blueberries.

Fill 6 separate 8-ounce ramekins with cobbler filling. Place on a parchment-lined sheet pan and distribute crumble topping evenly among ramekins.

Bake 10 minutes or until topping starts to brown and filling begins to bubble.

Serve warm with vanilla ice cream, drizzled with Fustini's Wild Blueberry Balsamic reduction.

Continued...

Crumble Topping:

2 cups all-purpose flour

¼ teaspoon salt

1¼ cups brown sugar

½ teaspoon ground cinnamon

1½ sticks cold, unsalted butter, cut into small cubes

1 whole egg and one egg yolk, beaten with ¼ cup milk

Place flour, salt, brown sugar, cinnamon and cubed butter in a mixing bowl.

With paddle attachment, slowly combine the ingredients until only tiny bits of butter remain visible.

With the mixer running at low speed, gradually pour in egg and milk mixture and blend just until clumps begin forming. It may not be necessary to add all of the liquid. Remove bowl from mixer and, with your fingers, mix the topping until it is a crumbly consistency.

Adapted from a recipe contributed by Amical, Traverse City

GREAT IDEAS:
- Drizzle on onions to caramelize in a sauté pan
- Drizzle on ice cream with fresh berries
- Reduce to use as syrup on waffles, pancakes or French toast
- Combine with Frantoio, Persian Lime or Meyer Lemon EVOO to make a delicious, fruity salad dressing
- Combine with Tuscan Herb or Basil EVOO for a sweet and savory marinade or salad dressing

SERVINGS VARY

Roasted Rhubarb Compote

8 cups rhubarb stalks, washed and cut into ¼-inch pieces

1½ cups granulated sugar

1 teaspoon cornstarch

2 tablespoons Fustini's Strawberry Balsamic, plus more for finishing

Heat oven to 350 degrees.

Place rhubarb on a sheet pan and toss with sugar to coat. Spread evenly and roast for 20–30 minutes or until soft when pierced with a fork. Remove from oven.

In a medium saucepan, combine cornstarch with 1 tablespoon rhubarb/sugar juices from roasting pan. Add in the rest of the pan juices, half of the roasted rhubarb and 2 tablespoons Fustini's Strawberry Balsamic and bring to a low boil. Cook mixture 5 minutes to thicken, stirring frequently. Add in the remaining roasted rhubarb and stir gently.

Serve over ice cream, Meyer Lemon Panna Cotta (recipe page 117) or Persian Lime-Pistachio Pound Cake (recipe page 118). Finish with a generous drizzle of Fustini's Strawberry Balsamic.

Adapted from a recipe contributed by Limonata, Holland

GREAT IDEAS:
- Combine with any Fustini's EVOO for great salad dressings
- Reduce and use as syrup on pancakes, waffles or French toast
- Drizzle over bruschetta instead of plain balsamic
- Great on ice cream with or without fresh berries
- Drizzle on cantaloupe and honeydew melon

FUSTINI'S
OILS & VINEGARS

STRAWBERRY
NATURAL STRAWBERRY FLAVORED
BALSAMIC VINEGAR

SERVES 6

Meyer Lemon Panna Cotta with Citrus Trio

2 cups whole milk

1½ cups heavy cream

½ cup white granulated sugar

zest of 1 lemon

½ cup Fustini's Meyer Lemon EVOO

2½ teaspoons unflavored gelatin

¼ cup cold water

1 cup mixed orange, lemon and grapefruit supremes

2 tablespoons Fustini's Grapefruit Balsamic

fresh mint sprigs

Note: In season, blood oranges may be substituted for regular oranges and Fustini's Blood Orange EVOO for Fustini's Meyer Lemon EVOO

Combine milk, cream, sugar and lemon zest in a medium saucepan. Bring to a boil over medium heat, stirring until sugar is dissolved. Remove pot from heat and pour Fustini's Meyer Lemon EVOO into the hot liquid.

Sprinkle gelatin over the cold water and stir to dissolve. Add completely dissolved gelatin to the hot liquid. Stir to combine thoroughly. Place the pan into a larger container filled with ice water. Stir occasionally to cool the mixture to room temperature. Once the mixture has cooled, use an electric hand mixer to emulsify the Fustini's Meyer Lemon EVOO into it.

Divide the mixture into six individual custard cups or molds and refrigerate overnight to set gelatin.

To unmold and serve, carefully dip bottom of each mold briefly in hot water. Run a thin knife around edge of each mold. Dry the outside of the mold and place serving plate on top of it. Invert mold and plate to release panna cotta. Serve with orange, lemon and grapefruit supremes that have been tossed in Fustini's Grapefruit Balsamic. Garnish with mint.

Adapted from a recipe contributed by Hanna Bistro, Traverse City

Persian Lime-Pistachio Pound Cake with Blueberry Compote

SERVES 6 – 8

1¼ cups flour

1 teaspoon baking powder

½ teaspoon salt

½ cup Fustini's Persian Lime EVOO

2 tablespoons whole milk

2 teaspoons fresh lime juice

2 large eggs

¾ cup granulated sugar

1 teaspoon lime zest, finely grated

4 tablespoons unsalted butter, melted and cooled

½ cup unsalted pistachios, chopped, plus more for garnish

whipped cream for garnish

....

Preheat oven to 350 degrees. Line bottom of an 8½ x 4½-inch loaf pan with parchment paper; butter paper and sides of pan.

Sift flour, baking powder and salt together into a bowl. In another bowl, whisk together Fustini's Persian Lime EVOO, milk and lime juice. Set flour mixture and oil mixture aside.

Fill a medium saucepan with 2 inches of water and bring to a simmer. In the bowl of an electric mixer, combine eggs, sugar and lime zest. Set bowl over saucepan of simmering water and whisk until egg mixture is warm to the touch, about 2 minutes. Transfer bowl to electric mixer fitted with whisk attachment. Beat on medium speed until mixture thickens, is pale yellow and forms ribbons when the whisk is lifted, 5–6 minutes.

When egg mixture has thickened, slowly drizzle in oil and milk mixture with the machine running. Reduce speed to low, add flour mixture and mix just to combine. Drizzle in butter and pistachios and mix, just to combine.

Pour batter into prepared pan. Bake, rotating pan once after 40 minutes, until top of cake is golden, the center bounces back when touched and a cake tester inserted in the center comes out clean, about 50 minutes. Unmold cake from pan and let cool completely on a wire rack. Serve with Blueberry Compote (recipe follows) and whipped cream, garnished with pistachios.

Blueberry Compote:

1 pint fresh blueberries, divided

¾ cup sugar

¼ cup water

¼ cup Fustini's Wild Blueberry Balsamic

½ teaspoon lime zest, finely grated

In a small saucepan, combine 1 cup of the blueberries, sugar, water and Fustini's Wild Blueberry Balsamic. Bring mixture to a boil and simmer about 5 minutes, until blueberries split and volume has reduced by about one quarter. Fold in remaining fresh blueberries and lime zest. Allow to cool.

GREAT IDEAS:
- Combine with Ginger and Honey or Grapefruit Balsamic to marinate shrimp, scallops, salmon, tuna or chicken
- Combine with any Fustini's balsamic for a great salad dressing or to grill fruit
- Use in baking in place of butter or other oils for brownies, cakes, breads or muffins
- Use to sauté shrimp and other shellfish

FUSTINI'S
OILS & VINEGARS

PERSIAN LIME
NATURAL PERSIAN LIME FLAVORED
EXTRA VIRGIN OLIVE OIL

SERVES 6

Strawberries with Balsamic Reduction and Mascarpone

2 pints fresh strawberries

12 ounces mascarpone cheese

4 tablespoons Fustini's 18 Year Traditional Balsamic

3 tablespoons sugar

mint leaves for garnish

. . . .

Wash, drain and stem strawberries and cut in half. Place in stainless steel bowl. Sprinkle with sugar and toss gently.

In six small, clear dessert bowls or martini glasses, place 2-ounce scoop of mascarpone cheese.

Add Fustini's 18 Year Traditional Balsamic to strawberries and toss gently but thoroughly. The sugars, juices and vinegar will form a rich, dark, almost chocolate-like syrup.

With a slotted spoon, evenly distribute the strawberries on top of mascarpone in bowls. Drizzle with the accumulated syrup. Garnish with mint leaves.

Contributed by Amical, Traverse City

GREAT IDEAS:
- Combine with any Fustini's citrus EVOO for salad dressing on a green salad with fresh strawberries, Roasted French Walnut Oil, mandarin orange slices and feta cheese
- Add to plain yogurt to flavor or drizzle over strawberry shortcake
- Combine with Chipotle or Tunisian Harissa EVOO to marinate salmon before grilling

"Better than Chocolate" Cupcakes

MAKES 18 CUPCAKES

1½ sticks butter (room temperature)

1⅔ cups sugar

3 large eggs

¼ cup Fustini's Vanilla Bean Balsamic

¼ cup Fustini's Chocolate Balsamic, divided, plus more for brushing

2 cups flour

⅔ cup Dutch-processed cocoa

1¼ teaspoon baking soda

¼ teaspoon baking powder

1 teaspoon salt

1⅓ cups water

. . . .

Preheat oven to 350 degrees.

Cream butter in a large mixing bowl. Add sugar, eggs and Fustini's Vanilla Bean Balsamic. Mix well, approximately 3 minutes on medium speed, scraping sides of bowl often. Sift dry ingredients together (flour, cocoa, baking soda, baking powder and salt) in a separate bowl. Add dry ingredients to the first bowl, alternating with the water (always begin and end with dry ingredients).

Fill cupcake liners ½ full. Add ½ teaspoon Fustini's Chocolate Balsamic to each filled liner and swirl into batter with a toothpick or the tip of a knife. Bake 20 minutes.

Remove cupcakes from oven and immediately poke holes in the top of each one. Using a pastry brush, liberally brush each cupcake with more chocolate balsamic. Cool on a wire rack.

When cooled, top each cupcake with your favorite buttercream frosting recipe. A fresh strawberry buttercream with fresh berries is recommended.

Contributed by Simply Cupcakes, Traverse City

Chocolate Espresso Pots de Crème

SERVES 6

2 cups whipping cream

1 cup whole milk

4 tablespoons Fustini's Espresso Bean Balsamic

4 tablespoons instant espresso powder

2 large eggs

6 large egg yolks

½ cup sugar

2 teaspoons pure vanilla extract

12 tablespoons chocolate shavings

whipped cream for garnish

4 tablespoons Ghirardelli chocolate syrup

cocoa powder for garnish

Callebaut chocolate recommended for shavings

Preheat oven to 300 degrees.

Scald milk, cream and Fustini's Espresso Bean Balsamic with espresso powder.

In a mixing bowl, mix together eggs, egg yolks, sugar and vanilla. Slowly add scalded liquid to the bowl. Mix without creating additional foam or air bubbles.

Fill 6 oven-safe cups or ramekins about ¾ full. Bake in a water bath 35–55 minutes, depending on heat and volume.

Cool, then top with shaved chocolate. Serve topped with whipped cream, chocolate syrup and cocoa powder.

Contributed by Amical, Traverse City

Techniques for Using Fustini's Oils & Vinegars

Marinate • Coat food in a mixture of Fustini's EVOO and balsamic and let it rest for a certain amount of time. The purpose of marinating is for the food to absorb the flavors of the marinade or, as in the case of a tough cut of meat, to tenderize it. Because most marinades contain acidic ingredients (4 percent in a dark balsamic and 6 percent in a white balsamic), the marinating should be done in a glass, ceramic or stainless steel container or in a ziplock bag—never in aluminum. For each pound of food to be marinated (meat, poultry, fish, vegetables), use 1 tablespoon each of EVOO and balsamic. Mix contents well and distribute evenly over food. Cover container. For best results, marinate for at least 1 hour, or up to 6 8 hours, in the refrigerator. Turn food halfway through marinating time. Remove food from the refrigerator at least 30-45 minutes before cooking and allow it to come to room temperature. Remove from marinade. Brush on any residual marinade during cooking. (Note: When fruits are similarly prepared, the term used is macerate.)

Emulsify • Slowly add Fustini's EVOO to a Fustini's balsamic while whisking vigorously. This disperses and suspends minute droplets of one liquid throughout the other. Emulsified mixtures are usually thick and satiny in texture. Emulsifying will allow you to evenly disperse a vinaigrette flavor over salads and fruit. For a vinaigrette, the usual ratio is 1:3 (e.g., 1 tablespoon balsamic to 3 tablespoons EVOO). You will notice that Fustini's EVOOs and balsamics hold together much better and longer in an emulsion than other oils and distilled vinegars.

Caramelize • Brush or drizzle any Fustini's balsamic on meat, fish, fruit or vegetables. Cook over medium heat in a pan coated with 1–2 tablespoons of Fustini's EVOO until the naturally occurring sugars in the balsamic become thicker and sticky, helping to brown (caramelize) the surface of the food.

Sauté • Cook food quickly in 1-2 tablespoons of Fustini's EVOO in a skillet or sauté pan over medium-high heat. Authentic EVOOs will withstand heat of up to 300–325 degrees.

Deglaze • After meat, poultry or fish has been sautéed in Fustini's EVOO and the food and any excess oil has been removed from the pan, deglazing is done by adding a small amount of Fustini's balsamic to the pan and stirring to loosen browned bits of food on the bottom. The mixture often becomes a sauce to accompany the food cooked in the pan.

Reduce • Bring Fustini's balsamic to a boil. Whisk constantly while maintaining a slow boil, until 50 percent of the volume is reduced by evaporation, thereby thickening the consistency and intensifying the flavor. Such a mixture is sometimes referred to as a reduction or a glaze and is used to finish both sweet and savory dishes.

BASIL

RECIPES on pages 3, 13, 58, 82, 94, 96

FLAVOR: Garden-fresh basil

COMPLEMENTS: Meats, salads, vegetables, breads, pastas

VINEGAR PAIRINGS: Asian Blackberry, Black Currant, Wild Blueberry, Chocolate, Cranberry, Ginger and Honey, Grapefruit, Lavender, Oregano, Peach, Golden Pineapple, Pomegranate, Peach, Raspberry, Strawberry, Sicilian Lemon, Tangerine, 18 Year Traditional

GREAT IDEAS:

- Brush on any fish before baking or grilling
- Drizzle over chopped fresh tomatoes for bruschetta and top with 18 Year Traditional Balsamic
- Combine with Strawberry, Raspberry or Lavender Balsamic for salad dressings
- Brush on bread for a grilled Caprese salad sandwich

BLOOD ORANGE

RECIPES on pages 26, 68, 117

FLAVOR: Fresh-fused citrus orange

COMPLEMENTS: Chicken, seafoods, salads, fruits, desserts, breads

VINEGAR PAIRINGS: Black Currant, Chocolate, Cinnamon Pear, Cranberry, Espresso Bean, Fig, Ginger and Honey, Jalapeño, Oregano, Raspberry, Red Apple, Sicilian Lemon, Strawberry, Tangerine, Vanilla Bean, 12 Year White, 18 Year Traditional

GREAT IDEAS:

- Combine with 18 Year Traditional Balsamic to marinate shrimp, scallops, salmon, pork or chicken
- Combine with any Fustini's balsamic for a great salad dressing
- Use in baking in place of butter or other oils for brownies, cakes or muffins

CHIPOTLE

RECIPES on pages 5, 28, 59, 61, 76

FLAVOR: Smoky and slightly spicy

COMPLEMENTS: Beef, poultry, pork, breads, pastas, vegetables

VINEGAR PAIRINGS: Asian Blackberry, Black Currant, Cherry, Chocolate, Cranberry, Cinnamon Pear, Espresso Bean, Fig, Jalapeño, Mango, Peach, Golden Pineapple, Pomegranate, Raspberry, Sicilian Lemon, Strawberry, Tangerine, Vanilla Bean, 18 Year Traditional

GREAT IDEAS:

- Combine with Espresso Bean or Chocolate Balsamic for a great marinade
- Brush on bread instead of butter for grilled cheese
- Combine with Strawberry Balsamic for a spicy, sweet and savory salad dressing
- Combine with Lavender Balsamic for Asian flavor
- Make salsa by combining with Tangerine Balsamic, chopped onions, tomatoes and cilantro for chips, chicken or pork

CILANTRO AND ONION

RECIPES on pages 6, 30, 61

FLAVOR: Roasted onion with a hint of cilantro

COMPLEMENTS: Chicken, eggs, salads, breads

VINEGAR PAIRINGS: Asian Blackberry, Black Currant, Fig, Lavender, Mango, Oregano, Peach, Pomegranate, Red Apple, Sicilian Lemon, Vanilla Bean, 18 Year Traditional

GREAT IDEAS:

- Combine with 18 Year Traditional Balsamic to marinate and grill chicken thighs
- Combine with Jalapeño Balsamic to marinate skirt steak for fajitas
- Use to roast cauliflower, broccoli, potatoes and asparagus
- Brush on bread for a grilled cheese sandwich

GARLIC

RECIPES on pages 5, 20, 33, 47, 56, 65, 81, 97, 103

FLAVOR: Fresh garlic

COMPLEMENTS: Salads, meats, seafoods, pastas, breads

VINEGAR PAIRINGS: Asian Blackberry, Champagne, Cherry, Cinnamon Pear, Coconut, Espresso Bean, Jalapeño, Mango, Oregano, Peach, Golden Pineapple, Pinot Noir, Red Apple, Sicilian Lemon, 12 Year White, 18 Year Traditional

GREAT IDEAS:

- Combine with 18 Year Traditional or Oregano Balsamic to drizzle on salads
- Combine with Peach or Golden Pineapple Balsamic for a chicken and pork marinade
- Combine with equal parts of Espresso Bean Balsamic and Tunisian Harissa EVOO for a flank steak or chicken marinade
- Use alone or with any Fustini's balsamic for roasting vegetables or bread dipping

MEYER LEMON

RECIPES on pages 2, 50, 93, 99, 117

FLAVOR: Fresh-fused citrus lemon

COMPLEMENTS: Chicken, seafoods, salads, fruits, vegetables, pastas, desserts, breads

VINEGAR PAIRINGS: Black Currant, Blueberry, Cherry, Chocolate, Cinnamon Pear, Cranberry, Espresso Bean, Ginger and Honey, Grapefruit, Lavender, Mango, Peach, Pinot Noir, Pomegranate, Raspberry, Red Apple, Sicilian Lemon, Strawberry, Tangerine, Vanilla Bean, 12 Year White, 18 Year Traditional

GREAT IDEAS:

- Combine with any Fustini's balsamic for salad dressing or roasting vegetables
- Use to sauté, bake or grill chicken, shrimp or fish
- Sauté dry rice in Meyer Lemon EVOO until translucent, add liquid, then cook as directed
- Replace other oils in baking

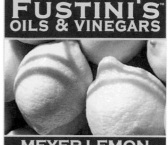

PERSIAN LIME

RECIPES on pages 6, 54, 66, 68, 103, 118

FLAVOR: Fresh Persian lime

COMPLEMENTS: Chicken, seafoods, salads, fruits, vegetables, desserts

VINEGAR PAIRINGS: Asian Blackberry, Blueberry, Cherry, Chocolate, Cinnamon Pear, Coconut, Cranberry, Fig, Ginger and Honey, Grapefruit, Jalapeño, Juniper Berry, Mango, Oregano, Golden Pineapple, Pinot Noir, Pomegranate, Raspberry, Red Apple, Sherry Reserva, Sicilian Lemon, Strawberry, Tangerine, Vanilla Bean, 12 Year White, 18 Year Traditional

GREAT IDEAS:

- Combine with Ginger and Honey or Grapefruit Balsamic to marinate shrimp, scallops, salmon, tuna or chicken
- Combine with any Fustini's balsamic for a great salad dressing or to grill fruit
- Use in baking in place of butter or other oils, i.e., brownies, cakes, breads or muffins
- Use to sauté shrimp and other shellfish

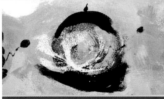

PORCINI MUSHROOM

RECIPE on page 12

FLAVOR: Porcini mushroom

COMPLEMENTS: Rice, risottos, beef, chicken, salads, vegetables, pastas, breads

VINEGAR PAIRINGS: Wild Blueberry, Champagne, Cherry, Fig, Oregano, Pomegranate, Sicilian Lemon, 18 Year Traditional

GREAT IDEAS:

- Use to sauté or roast vegetables
- Drizzle on pasta with prosciutto and caramelized red onions
- Brush on toast or English muffins
- Combine with Cherry Balsamic for spinach salad dressing
- Combine with Fig or Cherry Balsamic to marinate pork tenderloin or chicken
- Sauté chicken with Tunisian Harissa EVOO and Sicilian Lemon Balsamic

PROVENÇAL HERBES

RECIPES on pages 74, 104

FLAVOR: Light and savory, hints of rosemary, thyme, lavender, marjoram, fennel and bay leaf

COMPLEMENTS: Beef, pork, poultry, lamb, seafoods, rice, vegetables, potatoes, pastas

VINEGAR PAIRINGS: Asian Blackberry, Champagne, Coconut, Grapefruit, Lavender, Oregano, Golden Pineapple, Raspberry, Sherry Reserva, Tangerine, 12 Year White, 18 Year Traditional

GREAT IDEAS:

• Drizzle on pasta

• Use to cook rice or risotto

• Combine with Tangerine Balsamic to marinate poultry and pork

• Combine with Lavender Balsamic to marinate beef and lamb

• Use to roast potatoes and vegetables

• Great for bread dipping

• Combine with any Fustini's vinegar for a fresh-flavored green salad dressing

SAGE AND WILD MUSHROOM

RECIPE on page 86

FLAVOR: Savory sage with hints of shitake, chanterelle and morel mushrooms

COMPLEMENTS: Rice, vegetables, potatoes, pork, poultry, pastas, eggs

VINEGAR PAIRINGS: Asian Blackberry, Black Currant, Cherry, Cinnamon Pear, Cranberry, Juniper Berry, Lavender, Oregano, Peach, Golden Pineapple, Red Apple, Sicilian Lemon, 18 Year Traditional

GREAT IDEAS:

• Drizzle over noodles and smoked Gouda cheese

• Great for cooking omelets, frittatas, scrambled eggs

• Sauté dry rice in Sage and Wild Mushroom EVOO until translucent, add liquid, then cook as directed

• Use in place of butter for mashed potatoes

• Combine with Red Apple Balsamic to inject into and baste turkey

TARRAGON

RECIPE on page 70

FLAVOR: Subtle fresh tarragon

COMPLEMENTS: Chicken, seafoods, salads, pastas, breads, rice, vegetables

VINEGAR PAIRINGS: Coconut, Grapefruit, Lavender, Oregano, Golden Pineapple, Pinot Noir, Raspberry, Red Apple, Sicilian Lemon, 12 Year White, 18 Year Traditional

GREAT IDEAS:

• Combine with Grapefruit Balsamic to marinate chicken and seafood

• Use to cook rice and drizzle in Coconut Balsamic at the end for great flavoring

• Combine with any Fustini's balsamic for salad and add goat cheese, almonds and apples

• Sauté shrimp or scallops in Tarragon EVOO and finish with Sicilian Lemon Balsamic

TUNISIAN HARISSA

FLAVOR: Roasted chili peppers with hints of cumin, garlic, cinnamon and caraway

COMPLEMENTS: Meats, chicken, eggs, vegetables, breads, pastas

VINEGAR PAIRINGS: Black Currant, Wild Blueberry, Chocolate, Cinnamon Pear, Cranberry, Coconut, Espresso Bean, Grapefruit, Jalapeño, Mango, Peach, Golden Pineapple, Pinot Noir, Pomegranate, Raspberry, Sicilian Lemon, Strawberry, Tangerine, Vanilla Bean, 18 Year Traditional

GREAT IDEAS:

• Marinate with any Fustini's balsamic for grilling chicken, beef or pork

• Combine with Black Currant Balsamic to marinate salmon or shrimp

• Combine with Strawberry or Blueberry Balsamic for a spicy, sweet and savory dressing

• Use to cook fried or scrambled eggs and omelets

TUSCAN HERB

RECIPES on pages 14, 29, 77, 79

FLAVOR: A full-bodied blend of oregano, rosemary, sage and garlic with a peppery finish

COMPLEMENTS: Rice, risottos, beef, poultry, fish, vegetables, pastas, breads

VINEGAR PAIRINGS: Wild Blueberry, Champagne, Espresso Bean, Lavender, Oregano, Pinot Noir, Sicilian Lemon, 12 Year White, 12 Year Traditional, 18 Year Traditional

GREAT IDEAS:

- Great for sautéing, roasting or grilling vegetables, beef, pork, lamb, poultry or fish
- Drizzle on pasta and mix in prosciutto and caramelized red onions
- Combine with Lavender, 12 Year Traditional or 18 Year Traditional Balsamic for an excellent dressing
- Mix with grated Parmigiano Reggiano and 18 Year Traditional Balsamic for bread dipping

WHITE TRUFFLE

RECIPES on pages 9, 62, 74, 85, 86

FLAVOR: Earthy, buttery, mushroom, garlic, intense white truffle

COMPLEMENTS: Risotto, rice, sauces, vegetables

VINEGAR PAIRINGS: Sicilian Lemon, Tangerine

GREAT IDEAS:

- A finishing oil on steaks and potatoes, eggs and rice dishes
- Mix with Sicilian Lemon or Tangerine Balsamic for an unbelievable salad dressing

ARBEQUINA

RECIPE on page 62

FLAVOR: Sweet, buttery, light, fruity, reminiscent of fresh artichokes

COMPLEMENTS: Salads, vegetables, beef, chicken, fish, breads, vinaigrette dressings; an all-purpose oil

VINEGAR PAIRINGS: Black Currant, Champagne, Cranberry, Grapefruit, Juniper Berry, Lavender, Mango, Oregano, Peach, Golden Pineapple, Pinot Noir, Red Apple, Sicilian Lemon, Vanilla Bean, 12 Year White, 18 Year Traditional

GREAT IDEAS:

- Combine with any Fustini's balsamic for salad dressings or roasting/grilling/sautéing vegetables
- Use in place of other oils for baking
- Great for bread dipping

BARNEA

RECIPE on page 102

FLAVOR: Grassy with a fresh, peppery finish

COMPLEMENTS: Salads, vegetables, breads, vinaigrette dressings

VINEGAR PAIRINGS: Blueberry, Coconut, Oregano, 12 Year White, 18 Year Traditional

GREAT IDEAS:

- Combine with Coconut Balsamic and drizzle over fresh tomatoes or cucumbers
- Sauté fresh fish filets or chicken
- Drizzle over fingerling potatoes, then add sea salt and freshly cracked pepper and roast
- Combine with Wild Blueberry Balsamic for a great vinaigrette

FRANTOIO

RECIPES on pages 9, 25, 39, 92

FLAVOR: Full-bodied with a fresh, peppery finish

COMPLEMENTS: Salads, vegetables, breads, seafoods, pastas

VINEGAR PAIRINGS: Blueberry, Cherry, Cinnamon Pear, Fig, Juniper Berry, Oregano, Pinot Noir, 12 Year White, 18 Year Traditional

GREAT IDEAS:

- Combine with Sicilian Lemon Balsamic, drizzle over pasta, top with grated Asiago cheese and chopped fresh Roma tomatoes, add freshly cracked black pepper and toss
- Use to sauté or grill vegetables
- Combine with Pinot Noir Wine Vinegar, Dijon mustard, fresh garlic and basil for a great vinaigrette dressing

KORONEIKI

RECIPE on page 12

FLAVOR: Spicy, pungent, with a fresh peppery finish

COMPLEMENTS: Salads, vegetables, breads, vinaigrette dressings

VINEGAR PAIRINGS: Any white or dark balsamic, wine vinegar

GREAT IDEAS:

- Combine with Sicilian Lemon Balsamic and drizzle over thinly sliced fresh Brussels sprouts and pears; top with grated pecorino cheese, sea salt and pepper
- Sauté or grill vegetables
- Combine with Sherry Reserva Vinegar, Dijon mustard, fresh garlic and basil for a great vinaigrette

LECCINO

RECIPES on pages 9, 37, 41, 64, 84

FLAVOR: Full-bodied with a fresh, strong peppery finish

COMPLEMENTS: Salads, vegetables, chicken, seafoods, pastas, breads

VINEGAR PAIRINGS: Asian Blackberry, Grapefruit, Juniper Berry, Lavender, Oregano, Peach, Pinot Noir, Pomegranate, Raspberry, Sicilian Lemon, 12 Year White, 18 Year Traditional

GREAT IDEAS:

- Sauté asparagus, then drizzle with Lavender or Sicilian Lemon Balsamic
- Drizzle on peeled fresh beets, season with salt and pepper, wrap in foil and roast in oven
- Brush on shrimp kabobs, grill, then finish with Peach or Grapefruit Balsamic

MANZANILLO

RECIPES on pages 18, 66

FLAVOR: Sweet and buttery with a light, peppery finish

COMPLEMENTS: Salads, vegetables, chicken, seafoods, pastas, breads

VINEGAR PAIRINGS: Asian Blackberry, Juniper Berry, Oregano, Peach, Strawberry, Tangerine, 12 Year White, 18 Year Traditional

GREAT IDEAS:

- Sear chicken or tuna steaks in pan on both sides, remove from pan, reduce heat, then deglaze pan with Peach Balsamic and drizzle glaze over chicken or tuna
- Combine with Asian Blackberry Balsamic for a spinach and goat cheese salad dressing

PICHOLINE

RECIPES on pages 13, 42

FLAVOR: Mellow with hints of grassiness

COMPLEMENTS: Salads, vegetables, chicken, seafoods, pastas, breads

VINEGAR PAIRINGS: Cherry, Fig, Lavender, Oregano, Peach, Sicilian Lemon, Tangerine, 12 Year White or Dark, 18 Year Traditional

GREAT IDEAS:

- Drizzle on any fish before grilling or baking
- Combine with Cherry Balsamic and drizzle on goat cheese for a quick appetizer
- Combine with Oregano, 12 Year Traditional or 18 Year Traditional Balsamic for salads or pasta

PICUAL

RECIPES on pages 21, 22, 50

FLAVOR: Smooth, sweet, buttery, with a fresh peppery finish

COMPLEMENTS: Sauces, salads, vegetables, breads; good for sautéing and baking; all-purpose oil

VINEGAR PAIRINGS: Black Currant, Cranberry, Mango, Oregano, Peach, Golden Pineapple, Red Apple, Tangerine, 12 Year White or Dark, 18 Year Traditional

GREAT IDEAS:

- Combine with any Fustini's balsamic for salad dressings or roasting/grilling/sautéing vegetables
- Use in place of other oils for baking
- Great for bread dipping

137

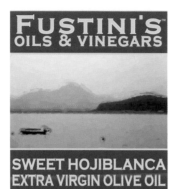

SWEET HOJIBLANCA

RECIPES on pages 22, 25, 46

FLAVOR: Mild, buttery, smooth with a fresh peppery finish

COMPLEMENTS: Salads, vegetables, beef, chicken, fish, breads, vinaigrette dressings; all-purpose oil

VINEGAR PAIRINGS: Champagne, Cranberry, Grapefruit, Oregano, Peach, Golden Pineapple, Raspberry, Red Apple, 12 Year White, 18 Year Traditional

GREAT IDEAS:

• Combine with any Fustini's balsamic for salad dressings or roasting/grilling/sautéing vegetables

• Sauté fresh fish filets or chicken

• Great for bread dipping

AVOCADO OIL

RECIPE on page 40

FLAVOR: Medium-bodied, smooth and buttery with the delicate flavor of avocado

COMPLEMENTS: Meats, seafoods, vegetables, vinaigrettes

VINEGAR PAIRINGS: Black Currant, Cranberry, Ginger and Honey, Grapefruit, Oregano, Sicilian Lemon, 18 Year Traditional

GREAT IDEAS:

- Use on rice or pasta
- Sauté carrots with Avocado Oil and top with Sicilian Lemon Balsamic to caramelize
- Great for avocado and goat cheese salads

ROASTED SESAME OIL

RECIPE on page 64

FLAVOR: Full-bodied, toasty and nutty

COMPLEMENTS: Chicken, seafoods, vegetables, salads, soups

VINEGAR PAIRINGS: Cinnamon Pear, Coconut, Fig, Golden Pineapple, Pomegranate, Red Apple, Sicilian Lemon, Tangerine

GREAT IDEAS:

- Combine with any Fustini's balsamic to marinate or grill chicken or seafood
- Drizzle on rice or pasta or add to oriental rice or noodle soup
- Combine with Basil EVOO to roast or sauté vegetables
- Use as finishing oil for Asian recipes

ROASTED FRENCH WALNUT OIL

RECIPE on page 49

FLAVOR: Warm roasted walnuts

COMPLEMENTS: Vegetables, salads, fruits, baked goods

VINEGAR PAIRINGS: Wild Blueberry, Cherry, Chocolate, Cinnamon Pear, Cranberry, Raspberry, Red Apple, Sicilian Lemon, 18 Year Traditional

GREAT IDEAS:

- Brush on whitefish or other fish before baking, sautéing or grilling
- Combine with any Fustini's balsamic for a salad dressing; particularly interesting combined with Red Apple Balsamic to dress a Waldorf salad
- Drizzle on oatmeal or brush on toast
- Use in pesto instead of pine nuts
- Use as a substitute for other oils or butter in baking
- Combine with Cinnamon Pear Balsamic to roast sweet potatoes

TOASTED PUMPKIN SEED OIL

FLAVOR: Toasted pumpkin seeds, nutty

COMPLEMENTS: Salads, vegetables, soups, breads

VINEGAR PAIRINGS: Cinnamon Pear, Jalapeño, Oregano, Pinot Noir, Red Apple, Strawberry, Sicilian Lemon, Vanilla Bean

GREAT IDEAS:

- Use as a salad dressing when combined with either a traditional or white balsamic
- Drizzle over butternut squash soup
- Brush on squash after baking
- Use as a finishing oil

ASIAN BLACKBERRY

RECIPE on page 68

FLAVOR: Sweet blackberries with a hint of ginger

COMPLEMENTS: Chicken, pork, seafoods, desserts, salads, fruits

OIL PAIRINGS: Basil, Chipotle, Garlic, Leccino, Manzanillo, Persian Lime, Provençal Herbes, Sage and Wild Mushroom

GREAT IDEAS:

- Combine with Garlic EVOO for grilled chicken and arugula salad
- Combine with Chipotle EVOO for beef, pork or chicken marinade
- Combine with Provençal Herbes EVOO for fruit salads or to drizzle on fruit kabobs
- Combine with Persian Lime or Basil EVOO for salad dressings

BLACK CURRANT

RECIPE on page 50

FLAVOR: Rich, dense black currant

COMPLEMENTS: Salads, fruits, meats

OIL PAIRINGS: Arbequina, Avocado, Basil, Blood Orange, Chipotle, Cilantro and Onion, Tunisian Harissa, Meyer Lemon, Picual, Sage and Wild Mushroom

GREAT IDEAS:

- Combine with Chipotle or Tunisian Harissa EVOO to marinate lamb, beef, pork or chicken when grilling
- Brush on pears, peaches and pineapples prior to grilling for great caramelization
- Combine with Blood Orange or Persian Lime EVOO for salad dressings
- Drizzle on ice cream and fresh berries

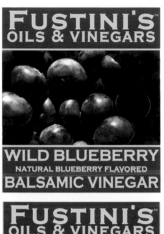

WILD BLUEBERRY

RECIPES on pages 41, 113, 119

FLAVOR: Rich, fruity and dense

COMPLEMENTS: Chicken, beef, pork, salads, fruits

OIL PAIRINGS: Barnea, Basil, Frantoio, Tunisian Harissa, Meyer Lemon, Persian Lime, Porcini, Tuscan Herb, Roasted French Walnut Oil

GREAT IDEAS:

- Drizzle on onions to caramelize in a sauté pan
- Drizzle on ice cream with fresh berries
- Reduce to use as syrup on waffles, pancakes or French toast
- Combine with Frantoio, Persian Lime or Meyer Lemon EVOO to make a delicious, fruity salad dressing
- Combine with Tuscan Herb or Basil EVOO for a sweet and savory marinade or salad dressing

CHERRY

RECIPES on pages 54, 62

FLAVOR: Rich, dense, sweet and tart at the same time

COMPLEMENTS: Salads, fruits, beef, chicken, pork, vegetables, ice creams, yogurts, cheeses

OIL PAIRINGS: Chipotle, Frantoio, Garlic, Meyer Lemon, Persian Lime, Picholine, Porcini, Sage and Wild Mushroom, Roasted French Walnut Oil

GREAT IDEAS:

- Use to marinate lamb, beef, pork roasts and chops for a caramelized surface
- Combine with Sage and Wild Mushroom EVOO to marinate chicken or pork
- Combine with Meyer Lemon EVOO for salad dressing
- Drizzle on a Caprese salad or bruschetta
- Drizzle on ice cream with fresh berries

CHOCOLATE

RECIPES on pages 57, 121

FLAVOR: Dark chocolate

COMPLEMENTS: Salads, fruits, chicken, pork, beef, desserts

OIL PAIRINGS: Basil, Blood Orange, Chipotle, Tunisian Harissa, Meyer Lemon, Persian Lime, Roasted French Walnut Oil

GREAT IDEAS:

- Combine with Chipotle or Tunisian Harissa EVOO for a Latin mole marinade for beef, pork and chicken
- Combine with Basil, Blood Orange, or Meyer Lemon EVOO for a great salad dressing
- Drizzle on fruit or ice cream

CINNAMON PEAR

RECIPES on pages 49, 57, 102, 110, 111

FLAVOR: Sweet, rich cinnamon with the hint of pears

COMPLEMENTS: Salads, fruits, desserts, pork, oatmeal

OIL PAIRINGS: Blood Orange, Chipotle, Frantoio, Garlic, Tunisian Harissa, Meyer Lemon, Persian Lime, Toasted Pumpkin Seed Oil, Sage and Wild Mushroom, Roasted Sesame Oil, Roasted French Walnut Oil

GREAT IDEAS:

- Combine with Blood Orange or Persian Lime EVOO for a salad dressing on spinach or arugula salad, then add fresh strawberries, Roasted French Walnut Oil, mandarin orange slices and feta cheese; or caramelize pears or apples and substitute goat cheese for feta
- Drizzle in yogurt, on ice cream or over apple crisp
- Use as a glaze on grilled salmon

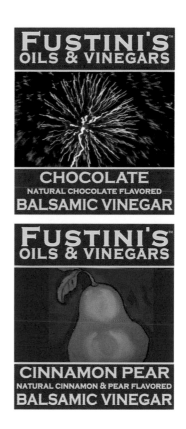

COCONUT

FLAVOR: Fresh, rich, creamy coconut

COMPLEMENTS: Salads, fruits, soups, vegetables, seafoods, chicken, pork, desserts

OIL PAIRINGS: Barnea, Garlic, Tunisian Harissa, Persian Lime, Provençal Herbes, Roasted Sesame Oil, Tarragon

GREAT IDEAS:

- Sauté shrimp in Persian Lime EVOO and finish with a drizzle of Coconut Balsamic
- Combine with Persian Lime EVOO and use as coleslaw dressing
- Caramelize baby carrots in a sauté pan
- Combine with Garlic EVOO for great Thai flavoring
- Combine with Provençal Herbes EVOO for a salad dressing
- Drizzle a little in a Mimosa

CRANBERRY

FLAVOR: Tart and fruity

COMPLEMENTS: Salads, fruits, chicken, pork, fish, water, adult beverages

OIL PAIRINGS: Arbequina, Avocado, Blood Orange, Chipotle, Tunisian Harissa, Hojiblanca, Meyer Lemon, Persian Lime, Picual, Sage and Wild Mushroom, Roasted French Walnut Oil

GREAT IDEAS:

- Combine with Persian Lime or Blood Orange EVOO or Roasted French Walnut Oil for a salad dressing
- Combine with Sage and Wild Mushroom, Chipotle or Tunisian Harissa EVOO for a marinade for chicken and pork
- Serve over ice with vodka or sparkling mineral water
- Use by itself as a glaze on salmon and tuna

ESPRESSO BEAN

RECIPES on pages 57, 122

FLAVOR: Rich, dark, sweet, with just the right amount of coffee flavor

COMPLEMENTS: Vegetables, salads, steaks, scallops, fruits, ice creams, desserts

OIL PAIRINGS: Blood Orange, Chipotle, Garlic, Tunisian Harissa, Meyer Lemon, Tuscan Herb

GREAT IDEAS:

- Combine with Tunisian Harissa or Chipotle EVOO and Garlic EVOO to marinate flank or skirt steaks; makes great fajitas

- Add to chili or baked beans as your "secret ingredient"

- Drizzle on fresh berries or ice cream

- For a great dessert, caramelize fresh pineapple chunks or brush on pears, peaches or pineapple rings, then grill

- Combine with Blood Orange EVOO for a pork tenderloin marinade

FIG

FLAVOR: Moderately tart

COMPLEMENTS: Salads, fruits, chicken, beef, pork, lamb, salmon, goat cheese

OIL PAIRINGS: Blood Orange, Chipotle, Cilantro and Onion, Frantoio, Persian Lime, Picholine, Porcini, Roasted Sesame Oil

GREAT IDEAS:

- Brush on cantaloupe or honeydew melon wedges, then top with chopped prosciutto and freshly grated Parmigiano Reggiano

- Combine with Chipotle EVOO, then brush on salmon, beef, chicken, or lamb chops prior to baking or grilling

- Combine with Blood Orange, Persian Lime or Porcini EVOO, then drizzle on a spinach salad with sliced water chestnuts and grapefruit slices

GINGER AND HONEY

RECIPES on pages 6, 46, 101

FLAVOR: Light and bright with intense ginger and subtle honey

COMPLEMENTS: Chicken, pork, salads, fruits, seafoods, rice

OIL PAIRINGS: Avocado, Basil, Blood Orange, Meyer Lemon, Persian Lime

GREAT IDEAS:

- Marinate cucumbers or water chestnuts in Ginger and Honey Balsamic and serve alone or add to salad
- Sear tuna or salmon in any Fustini's EVOO, then deglaze pan with Ginger and Honey Balsamic and drizzle glaze over fish
- Use in stir-fry dishes
- Flavor rice
- Great on fruit salads or green salads
- Add to bottled or sparkling water for refreshing flavor

GOLDEN PINEAPPLE

RECIPE on page 66

FLAVOR: Light and sweet, fresh golden pineapple

COMPLEMENTS: Salads, fruits, pork, seafoods, desserts

OIL PAIRINGS: Arbequina, Basil, Chipotle, Garlic, Tunisian Harissa, Hojiblanca, Persian Lime, Picual, Provençal Herbes, Sage and Wild Mushroom, Roasted Sesame Oil, Tarragon

GREAT IDEAS:

- Combine with Garlic or Chipotle EVOO to marinate flank steak or pork tenderloin before grilling
- Drizzle into cooked rice, then add broccoli, carrots, green pepper and your favorite meat or seafood
- Use with any Fustini's EVOO for a great salad dressing
- Combine with Tarragon EVOO and brush on tuna or other fish before grilling or baking

GRAPEFRUIT

RECIPE on page 117

FLAVOR: Sweet, pink grapefruit, only better!

COMPLEMENTS: Salads, fruits, seafood, chicken, pork, rice

OIL PAIRINGS: Arbequina, Avocado, Basil, Provençal Herbes, Tunisian Harissa, Hojiblanca, Leccino, Meyer Lemon, Persian Lime, Tarragon

GREAT IDEAS:

- Combine with Provençal Herbes EVOO and drizzle on spinach salad with grapefruit or tangerine pieces, a drizzle of Roasted French Walnut Oil and some dried cherries
- Combine with Tarragon EVOO in a marinade for chicken or fish
- Use with any Fustini's EVOO to flavor rice
- Drizzle on a fruit salad
- Use to flavor bottled or sparkling water

JALAPEÑO

RECIPES on pages 5, 40

FLAVOR: Zesty jalapeño with a touch of heat

COMPLEMENTS: Salads, beef, chicken, pork, vegetables

OIL PAIRINGS: Blood Orange, Chipotle, Garlic, Tunisian Harissa, Persian Lime, Toasted Pumpkin Seed Oil

GREAT IDEAS:

- Combine with Chipotle, Tunisian Harissa or Persian Lime EVOO for an exceptional marinade for chicken thighs and wings
- Drizzle over redskin potato and green bean salads
- Combine with Blood Orange or Persian Lime EVOO for a great fajita marinade
- Drizzle over steamed vegetables or on any salad
- Excellent on sliced tomatoes or beets

JUNIPER BERRY

FLAVOR: Sweet beginning with a tart finish

COMPLEMENTS: Salads, fruits, chicken, pork, wild game

OIL PAIRINGS: Arbequina, Frantoio, Leccino, Manzanillo, Persian Lime, Sage and Wild Mushroom

GREAT IDEAS:

- Combine with Frantoio or any Fustini's Single Varietal EVOO for a Bibb lettuce salad with mushrooms marinated in Juniper Berry Balsamic
- Combine with Provençal Herbes or Tuscan Herb EVOO to marinate venison or any other wild game, or with Sage and Wild Mushroom EVOO for a great pork marinade
- Drizzle over Brussels sprouts that have been sautéed in Meyer Lemon EVOO

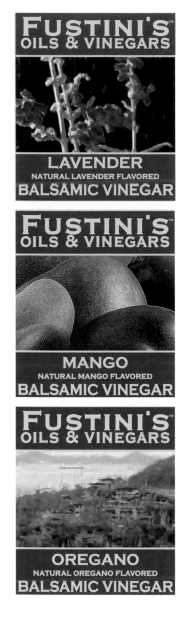

LAVENDER

FLAVOR: Rich and peppery with a hint of lavender; very elegant

COMPLEMENTS: Salads, fruits, beef, chicken, pork, lamb, vegetables

OIL PAIRINGS: Arbequina, Basil, Chipotle, Cilantro and Onion, Leccino, Meyer Lemon, Picholine, Provençal Herbes, Sage and Wild Mushroom, Tarragon, Tuscan Herb

GREAT IDEAS:

• Combine with Tuscan Herb EVOO and use as a marinade on chicken, beef, pork, lamb or fish

• Roast vegetables or drizzle on steamed vegetables

• Combine with any Fustini's EVOO for great salad dressings

• Drizzle on fruit or ice cream

MANGO

RECIPE on page 66

FLAVOR: Fruity with floral notes, slightly sweet

COMPLEMENTS: Fruits, salads, chicken, pork, fish

OIL PAIRINGS: Arbequina, Chipotle, Cilantro and Onion, Garlic, Tunisian Harissa, Meyer Lemon, Persian Lime, Picual

GREAT IDEAS:

• Combine with any Fustini's citrus EVOO for a sweet but crisp vinaigrette

• Combine with any Fustini's EVOO for a grilling marinade

• Brush on grilled fruit before removing from heat

• Use with Chipotle or Tunisian Harissa EVOO for a fruity salsa

OREGANO

RECIPES on pages 21, 37, 82, 94

FLAVOR: Very fresh oregano

COMPLEMENTS: Salads, tomatoes, cucumbers, beef, chicken, fish

OIL PAIRINGS: Basil, Blood Orange, Cilantro and Onion, Garlic, Persian Lime, Porcini, Toasted Pumpkin Seed Oil, Sage and Wild Mushroom, Tarragon, Tuscan Herb, any Single Varietal EVOO

GREAT IDEAS:

• Combine with Blood Orange EVOO, then drizzle on a Caprese salad

• Combine with Porcini, Basil or Garlic EVOO, then drizzle over pasta or use as a great salad dressing

• Chop tomatoes and cucumber, drizzle in Oregano Balsamic and add salt and pepper for savory bruschetta

PEACH

RECIPES on pages 47, 56, 113

FLAVOR: Light and sweet, like fresh peaches

COMPLEMENTS: Salads, fruits, pork, fish, seafoods

OIL PAIRINGS: Arbequina, Basil, Chipotle, Garlic, Tunisian Harissa, Hojiblanca, Leccino, Manzanillo, Meyer Lemon, Picholine, Picual, Sage and Wild Mushroom

GREAT IDEAS:

- Marinate sliced cucumbers and top with sea salt and freshly ground pepper
- Combine with Basil or Meyer Lemon EVOO for a great salad dressing
- Combine with Garlic, Tunisian Harissa or Chipotle EVOO to marinate pork tenderloin or chicken
- Add to bottled water or sparkling mineral water for a refreshing thirst quencher

POMEGRANATE

FLAVOR: Medium tart

COMPLEMENTS: Salads, lamb, beef, chicken, duck

OIL PAIRINGS: Basil, Chipotle, Tunisian Harissa, Leccino, Meyer Lemon, Persian Lime, Porcini, Roasted Sesame Oil

GREAT IDEAS:

- Use to caramelize red onions
- Combine with Persian Lime, Meyer Lemon or Basil EVOO and serve over salad greens topped with nuts, feta cheese and caramelized red onion
- Combine with Basil EVOO to marinate lamb or duck
- Reduce in a saucepan and drizzle over strawberries or duck

RASPBERRY

FLAVOR: Medium tart

COMPLEMENTS: Vegetables, fruits, salads, pork, poultry

OIL PAIRINGS: Basil, Blood Orange, Chipotle, Tunisian Harissa, Leccino, Meyer Lemon, Persian Lime, Provençal Herbes, Tarragon, Roasted French Walnut Oil

GREAT IDEAS:

- Reduce for a chicken breast glaze with dash of oregano, grape jelly and black pepper
- Combine with Basil EVOO, then drizzle over baby greens with goat cheese and toasted pecans
- Reduce and use as syrup on pancakes, waffles and French toast
- Combine with Provençal Herbes EVOO and drizzle over fruit skewers

FUSTINI'S
OILS & VINEGARS

PEACH
NATURAL PEACH FLAVORED
BALSAMIC VINEGAR

FUSTINI'S
OILS & VINEGARS

POMEGRANATE
NATURAL POMEGRANATE FLAVORED
BALSAMIC VINEGAR

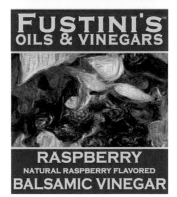

FUSTINI'S
OILS & VINEGARS

RASPBERRY
NATURAL RASPBERRY FLAVORED
BALSAMIC VINEGAR

RED APPLE

RECIPES on pages 102, 110

FLAVOR: Sweet apple

COMPLEMENTS: Salads, fruits, pork, poultry

OIL PAIRINGS: Arbequina, Blood Orange, Cilantro and Onion, Garlic, Hojiblanca, Meyer Lemon, Persian Lime, Picual, Toasted Pumpkin Seed Oil, Sage and Wild Mushroom, Sesame, Tarragon, Roasted French Walnut Oil

GREAT IDEAS:

- Combine with Sage and Wild Mushroom EVOO to baste and inject into turkey
- Drizzle on sweet potatoes and roast
- Drizzle on apple crisp
- Combine with Roasted French Walnut Oil, Garlic EVOO or Toasted Pumpkin Seed Oil for salad dressing
- Combine with Cilantro and Onion EVOO, then brush on acorn squash before baking

SICILIAN LEMON

RECIPES on pages 10, 65, 81, 101

FLAVOR: Bright, fresh, and slightly sweet lemon

COMPLEMENTS: Salads, fruits, seafoods, vegetables, pastas

OIL PAIRINGS: Basil, Blood Orange, Chipotle, Cilantro and Onion, Garlic, Tunisian Harissa, Meyer Lemon, Persian Lime, Porcini, Sage and Wild Mushroom, Tarragon, Tuscan Herb, all EVOOs and Specialty Oils

GREAT IDEAS:

- Combine with Basil or Garlic EVOO for a great marinade for vegetables and seafoods
- Combine with Basil EVOO and drizzle over fresh pasta, then add chopped, fresh tomatoes and freshly grated Asiago cheese
- Combine with Meyer Lemon EVOO for roasting asparagus or drizzling on steamed vegetables
- Combine with Picholine or Arbequina EVOO for a light and bright salad dressing or drizzle on sliced tomatoes
- Drizzle on fruit salads or add to sparkling water

STRAWBERRY

RECIPE on page 115

FLAVOR: Sweet, summer strawberries

COMPLEMENTS: Salads, fruits, desserts

OIL PAIRINGS: Basil, Blood Orange, Chipotle, Tunisian Harissa, Manzanillo, Meyer Lemon, Persian Lime, Toasted Pumpkin Seed Oil

GREAT IDEAS:

- Combine with any Fustini's EVOO for great salad dressings
- Reduce and use as syrup on pancakes, waffles or French toast
- Drizzle over bruschetta instead of plain balsamic
- Great on ice cream with or without fresh berries
- Drizzle on cantaloupe and honeydew melon

TANGERINE

RECIPES on pages 5, 42, 64

FLAVOR: Fresh citrus

COMPLEMENTS: Vegetables, salads, chicken, fish

OIL PAIRINGS: Basil, Blood Orange, Chipotle, Tunisian Harissa, Manzanillo, Meyer Lemon, Persian Lime, Picholine, Picual, Provençal Herbes, Roasted Sesame Oil

GREAT IDEAS:

- Combine with Meyer Lemon or Blood Orange EVOO as a tasty glaze for baked or grilled salmon
- Combine with Persian Lime for a zesty salad dressing
- Combine with Chipotle or Tunisian Harissa EVOO for a great marinade on chicken, beef or pork
- Slice apples and caramelize with Tangerine Balsamic in sauté pan, then serve over pound cake for a quick and easy dessert

VANILLA BEAN

RECIPES on pages 8, 121

FLAVOR: Sweet, creamy vanilla bean

COMPLEMENTS: Salads, fruits, desserts

OIL PAIRINGS: Arbequina, Blood Orange, Chipotle, Cilantro and Onion, Tunisian Harissa, Meyer Lemon, Persian Lime, Toasted Pumpkin Seed Oil

GREAT IDEAS:

- Combine with any Fustini's citrus EVOO for dressing a green salad with fresh strawberries, Roasted French Walnut Oil, mandarin orange slices and feta cheese.
- Add to plain yogurt to flavor or drizzle over strawberry shortcake
- Combine with Chipotle or Tunisian Harissa EVOO to marinate salmon before grilling

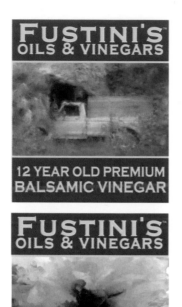

12 YEAR TRADITIONAL

RECIPES on pages 12, 79, 104

FLAVOR: Crisp, savory and dense; a little sharper than the 18 Year Traditional

COMPLEMENTS: Fruits, salads, desserts

OIL PAIRINGS: Pair with any Fustini's EVOO

GREAT IDEAS:

- Use a splash in soups and on seafood
- Combine with Garlic, Tuscan Herb or Provençal Herbes EVOO for a savory salad dressing
- Combine with Meyer, Lemon, Persian Lime or Blood Orange EVOO for a tart citrus dressing on salads or for roasting asparagus, Brussels sprouts or green beans

12 YEAR WHITE

RECIPES on pages 2, 30, 58, 97

FLAVOR: Crisp, clear and slightly sweet

COMPLEMENTS: Fruits, salads, white fish

OIL PAIRINGS: Blood Orange, Garlic, Meyer Lemon, Persian Lime, Provençal Herbes, Tarragon, Tuscan Herb, any Fustini's Single Varietal EVOO

GREAT IDEAS:

- Combine with any Fustini's citrus EVOO and drizzle on a wedge of lettuce with fresh tomato slices and blue cheese or Gorgonzola cheese
- Combine with Garlic EVOO, drizzle over green beans and serve warm or chilled
- Drizzle over fresh fruit salad
- Brush on any white fish, sprinkle on fresh thyme and bake

18 YEAR TRADITIONAL

RECIPES on pages 14, 76, 92, 120

FLAVOR: Classically sweet

COMPLEMENTS: Salads, soups, fruits, beef, chicken, pork, breads

OIL PAIRINGS: Any Fustini's EVOO pairs well with this traditional and
sweet balsamic

GREAT IDEAS:

- Combine with Chipotle or Tunisian Harissa EVOO for grilling
- Drizzle over steamed or roasted vegetables
- Drizzle on bruschetta or Caprese salad
- Drizzle over fruit or ice cream
- Combine with any Fustini's EVOO for bread dipping

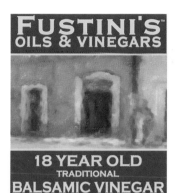

CHAMPAGNE VINEGAR

RECIPES on pages 84, 103

FLAVOR: Champagne

COMPLEMENTS: Salads, pork

OIL PAIRINGS: Arbequina, Garlic, Hojiblanca, Porcini, Provençal Herbes, Tuscan Herb

GREAT IDEAS:

- Called for in many salad dressing and sauce recipes
- Combine with Sweet Hojiblanca EVOO for a nice balance of sweet and sharp
- Combine with Provençal Herbes EVOO for a tangy vinaigrette
- Add to any Fustini's balsamic, like Strawberry, for extra zest

PINOT NOIR WINE VINEGAR

RECIPES on pages 37, 39

FLAVOR: Pinot Noir wine

COMPLEMENTS: Salads, vegetables, pork, beef, soups, marinades

OIL PAIRINGS: Arbequina, Frantoio, Garlic, Tunisian Harissa, Leccino, Meyer Lemon, Persian Lime, Toasted Pumpkin Seed Oil, Tarragon, Tuscan Herb

GREAT IDEAS:

- Combine with any Fustini's EVOO for a great salad dressing
- Combine with Tunisian Harissa EVOO and drizzle over green beans
- Combine with Arbequina or Tuscan Herb EVOO to marinate olives
- Marinate chicken thighs with Pinot Noir Vinegar, Tunisian Harissa EVOO or Persian Lime EVOO (or all three together) for exceptional flavor
- Add to potato salads with green beans and caramelized onions
- Use in any recipe calling for red wine vinegar

SHERRY RESERVA VINEGAR

RECIPES on pages 8, 18

FLAVOR: Aged Sherry

COMPLEMENTS: Most salads

OIL PAIRINGS: Persian Lime, Provençal Herbes

GREAT IDEAS:

- Combine with Persian Lime EVOO for dressing taco salad
- Combine with Provençal Herbes EVOO for a savory salad dressing
- Add to gazpacho for enhanced flavor
- Marinate olives in Sherry Reserva Vinegar, Sweet Hojiblanca EVOO, fresh orange juice, lemon zest, garlic and thyme
- Great mixed with our 18 Year Traditional Balsamic to add a sharper note

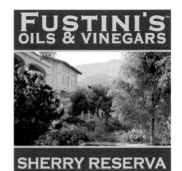